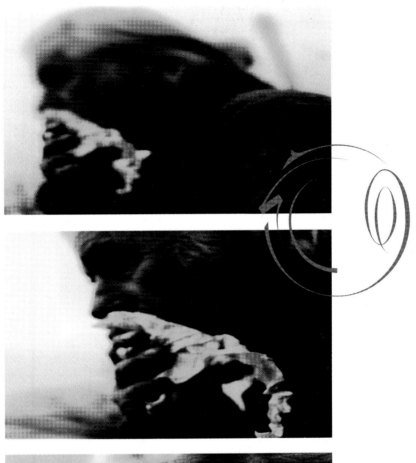

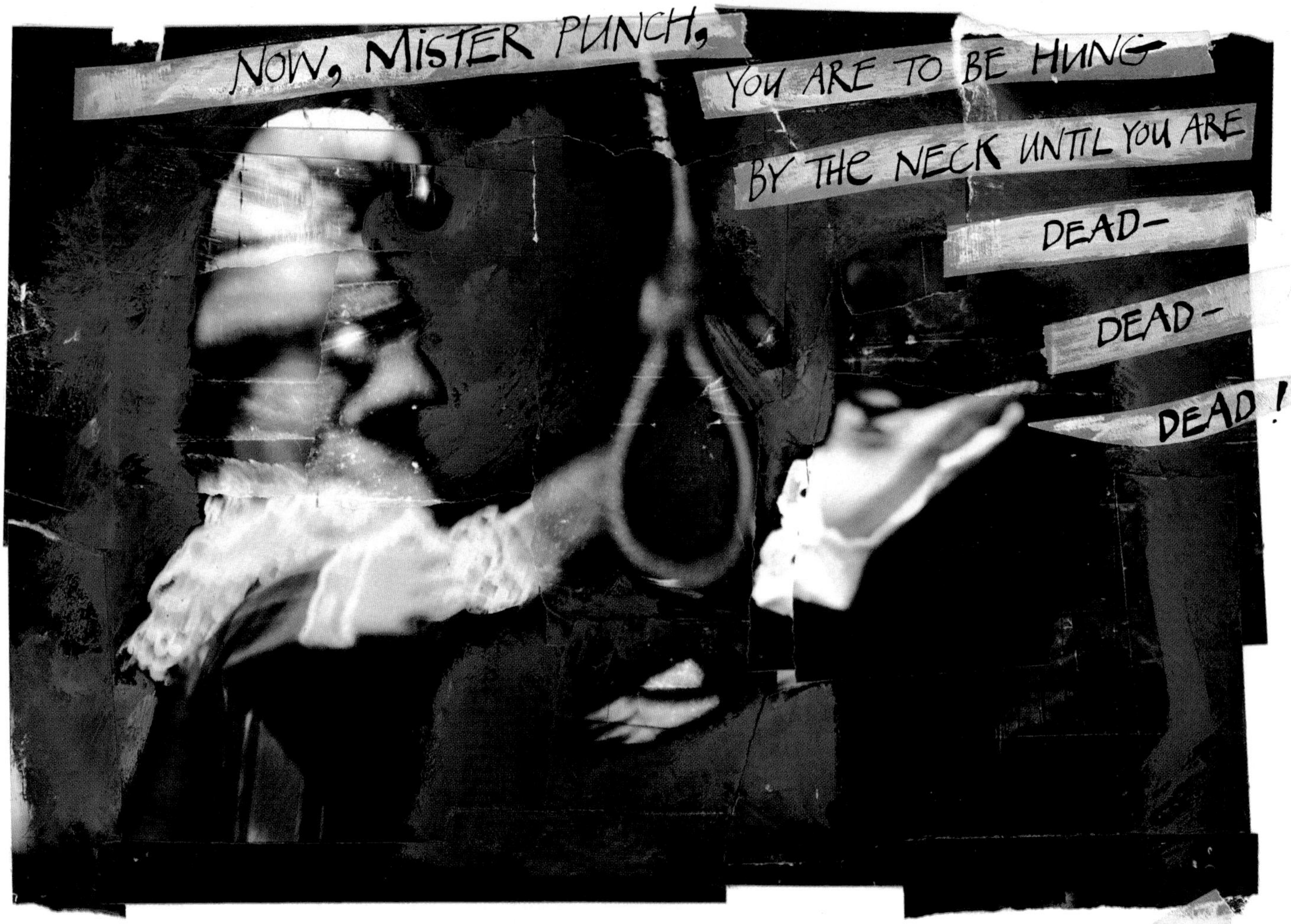
NOW, MISTER PUNCH,
YOU ARE TO BE HUNG
BY THE NECK UNTIL YOU ARE
DEAD—
DEAD—
DEAD!

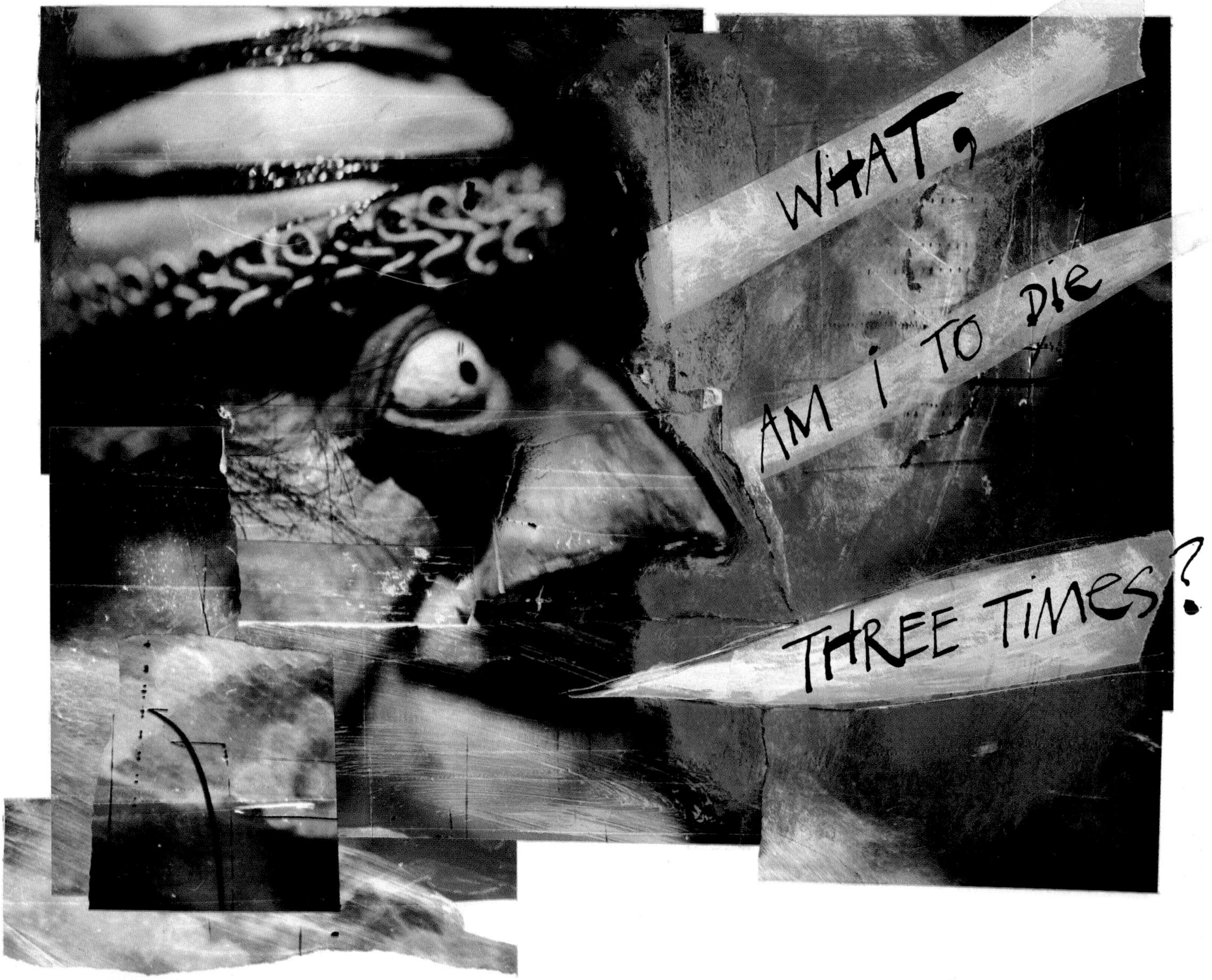
WHAT,
AM I TO DIE
THREE TIMES?

ACKNOWLEDGEMENT

Thank you to my parents and Aunts and Uncles, whose memories, both of Punch and Judy, and of my family history, I have so recklessly and shamelessly plundered and twisted to my own purposes.

Thank you to the readers and critics of this story in its various drafts, particularly Dave McKean, Martha Soukup and Steve Brust, and, with especially grateful appreciation for his critical faculties and accurate advice, John Clute.

Thank you to Faith Brooker, for her patience and faith; to Merrilee Heifetz and Carole Blake for their work behind the scenes.

Thank you to Kathleen O'Shea, and the Atlanta Centre for Puppetry Arts.

And a final thank you to all the working Professors, past and present, for the lessons of their tragical comedy.

Neil.

Thanks to Christopher and Andrew Waring, Geoffrey Scott, Ken and Eileen Lowes, Garth, Delia, Clare and Louise Haythornthwaite, and Nora McKean.

Also thanks to Bob Watt, Malcolm Hatton and all at Splash of Paint Design.

Dave.

DEDICATION

For Holly Gaiman, who is now too old to be thrown out of the window and for Yolanda McKean, who is just the right age.
And for all the other new cast members who joined us during the preparation and completion of this book including Sky McCloud, Nikolai Muth, Ambre Mattotti, Emily DeFiore, Zachary Bruning...

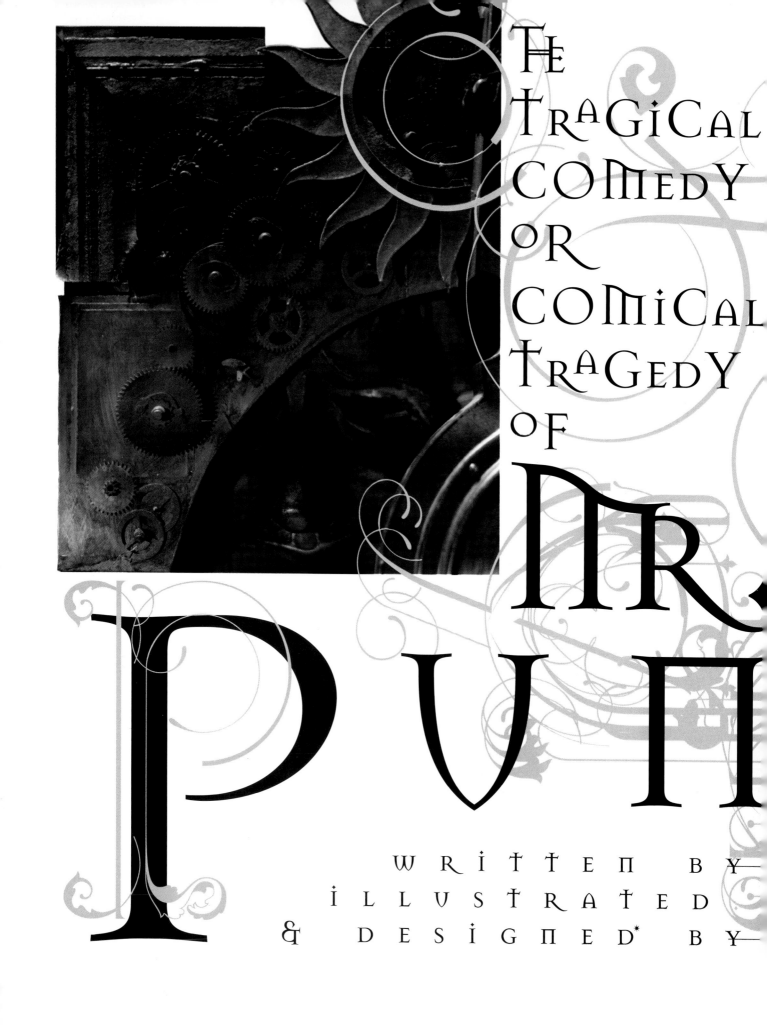

THE
TRAGICAL
COMEDY
OR
COMICAL
TRAGEDY
OF

MR
PUH

WRITTEN BY
ILLUSTRATED
& DESIGNED* BY

FONTS BY
DAVE McKEAN
AND EMIGRE

C H A ROMANCE

NEIL GAIMAN
DAVE McKEAN

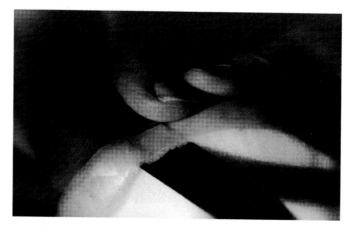

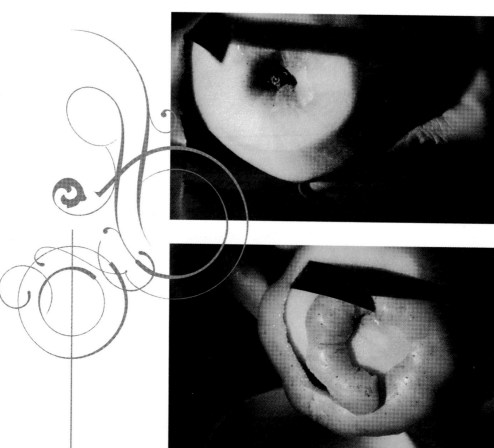

Published by DC Comics 1995 under license with Victor Gollancz Ltd. First published in Great Britain 1994 by Victor Gollancz.

Copyright © 1994 Neil Gaiman and Dave McKean.

First paperback edition 1995.

Vertigo is a trademark of DC Comics.

DC Comics, 1700 Broadway
New York, NY 10019
A Warner Bros. Entertainment Company

Printed in Canada. Fifth printing.

isbn: 1-56389-246-4.

This edition intended for sale in the United States and Canada only.

My grandfather Arthur once took me fishing. I was seven.

I suppose he must have gone fishing frequently, although i never recall him bringing back any fish, nor indeed, any other fishing trips.

He woke me up at five, before the sun was up.

It was late summer; a cold, hard rain had been slashing down for the previous week. It was not raining that morning, although it was very, very cold.

Together we walked, in the darkness, down to the seafront. I carried one set of rods in a brown canvas case; he carried the other, together with a mass of squirming maggots, floats, weights, sandwiches, and a thermos of home-made soup, all in a small wicker basket. He also carried a folding stool.

We walked down to the beach
until we reached the sea.

My face and hands were chilled, but I'd been bundled
up warmly by my grandmother before i left the house.

We set up the rods — baiting our hooks with
maggots, casting off, and waiting, in the night.

I listened to the waves
pound on the pebbles.

After a while the
sky began to grey,
and i realised i
had had enough
of fishing.

The beach was empty, my arms were tired, and this
had gone on too long. We'd caught nothing. I
wondered why the fish were ignoring our bait: the
thick, sandy maggots that my grandfather had impaled
with such care. Wasn't it just what they wanted?

grandfather sat on his cloth stool, patient and waiting.
I reeled in my line, and left the fishing rod on the pebbles.

Don't go
too far

advised my grandfather Arthur.

At that time in the morning the beach was empty.
There were no other fishermen, no early morning
walkers (the jogger would not appear for another
decade; indeed, my grandmother had pointed out
to me my first hippy, whom she referred to as a
beatnik, only the week before).

The pre-dawn world lacked colour; there was
grey in abundance and a strange strained blue.

But there was one patch of colour on the
beach, and it was that i walked towards.

Hip Pip Poy.

Hip Pip Poy.

I walked around the
back and looked inside.
It was empty.

I'm coming.

I'm coming.

Ooooooh I'm coming.

I won't be a minute
little boys and girls.

Where's Judy?

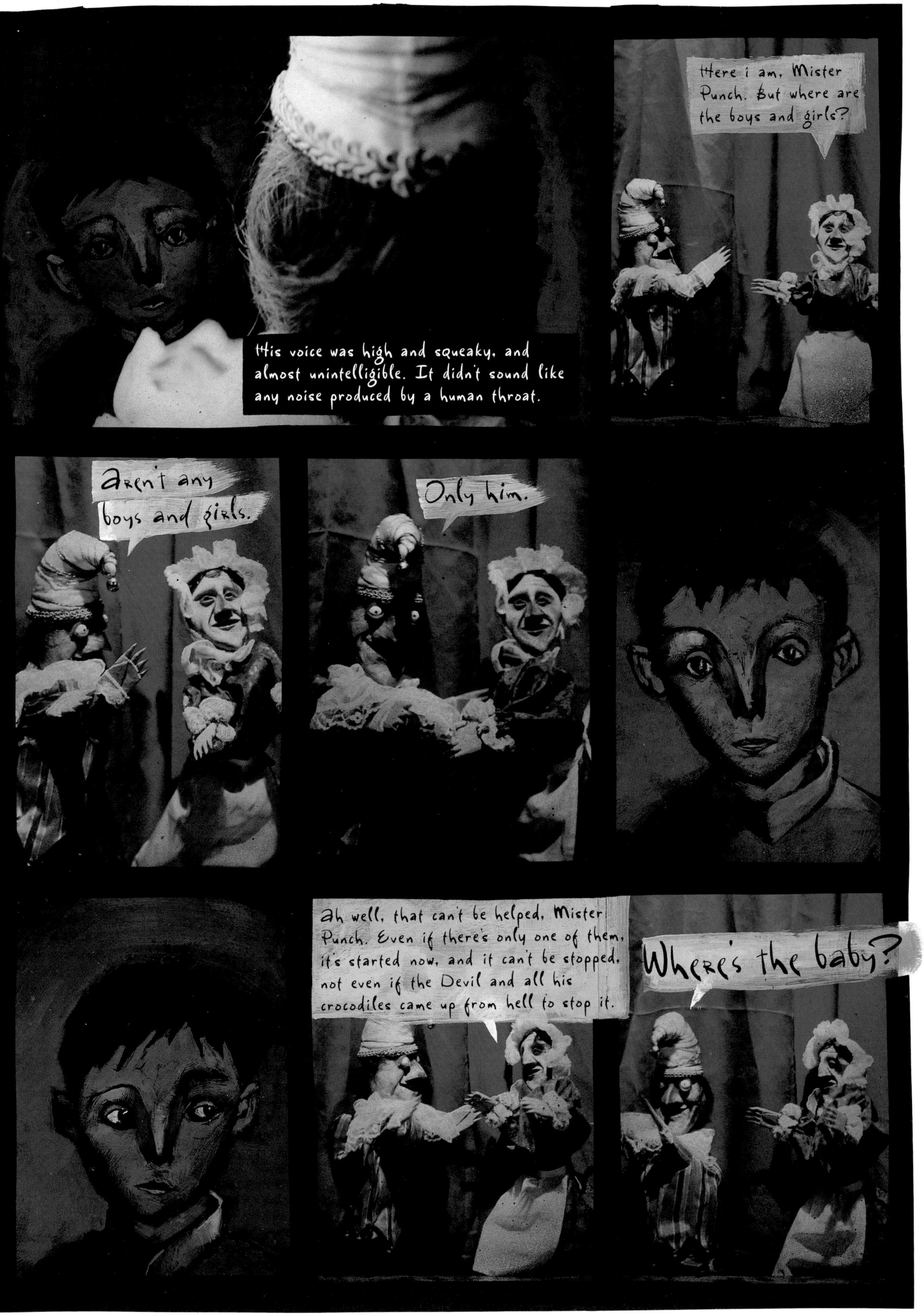
His voice was high and squeaky, and almost unintelligible. It didn't sound like any noise produced by a human throat.
Here i am, Mister Punch. But where are the boys and girls?
aren't any boys and girls.
Only him.
ah well, that can't be helped, Mister Punch. Even if there's only one of them, it's started now, and it can't be stopped, not even if the Devil and all his crocodiles came up from hell to stop it.
Where's the baby?

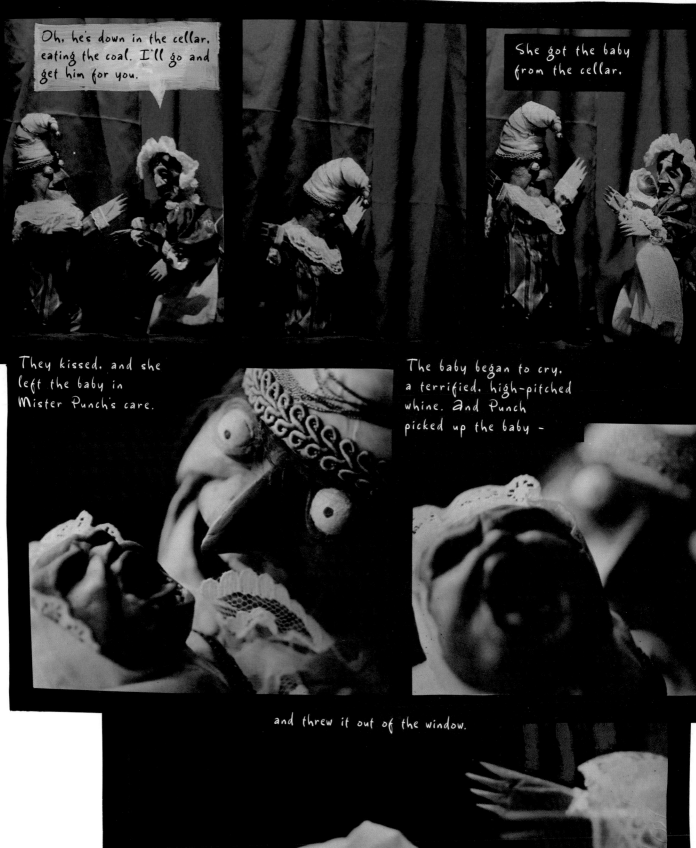

Oh, he's down in the cellar, eating the coal. I'll go and get him for you.

She got the baby from the cellar.

They kissed, and she left the baby in Mister Punch's care.

The baby began to cry, a terrified, high-pitched whine. And Punch picked up the baby –

and threw it out of the window.

Not really.

He didn't throw it out of the window.

He threw it off the stage.

It tumbled down from the stage onto the beach—

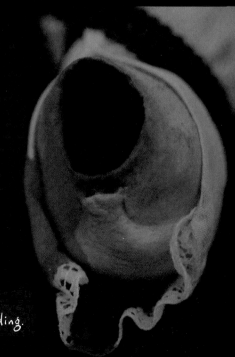

and lay there, silent and bleeding.

The puppets lay, tiny and flaccid and still on the front board.

I stopped and turned when i reached the water's edge.

My grandfather still sat on his collapsible stool, with the line taut out to sea. His wicker basket sat open beside him. He had caught nothing.

It began to rain, and we went back to my grandparents' house.

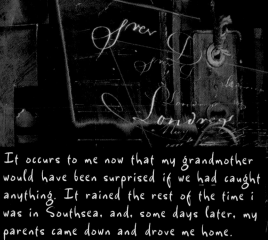

It occurs to me now that my grandmother would have been surprised if we had caught anything. It rained the rest of the time i was in Southsea, and, some days later, my parents came down and drove me home.

I am lonely   now   and very   far from home.

I find myself grasping for my roots, awkwardly. And i wonder what my grandparents would think of me, were they to meet me today. Ask their shades about me and i imagine they would pull fumbling ghost photographs from their wallets and handbags, show you a small solemn child with huge hazel eyes:

"I'm afraid he's a bit of a handful." they'd say.

for them (no matter how dead they are; and death is relative, not absolute. You can be slightly dead, just as you can be slightly pregnant). for my grandparents, i will always be a small boy.

I also have my mental snapshots of them: frozen moments of the past, in which the dead are captured in tiny loops of motion.

I play them now, in my mind:

1972: My father's father, on day-release from the mad-house, on the seafront at Southsea, coughing thick grey phlegm into a paper handkerchief. his voice a low and bitter growl.

1977: My mother's father, Arthur, ten years after our fishing trip, his white eyebrows bushy and wild. lost and tearful and stammering, having been brought back by neighbours following another wander down the road.

1979: My mother's mother, Ruby, a few days before her death: looking at her and realising that she had somehow become fragile and paper-thin, a ghost, no longer a tough old bird.

1986: My father's mother, the only person to whom i have ever said goodbye, properly, before they died: I remember her holding a paring knife, and peeling apples before she sliced and ate them. Her hands: red, and wet, and arthritic; the apple peel curling onto newspaper in her lap. Also i remember the tart taste of the apples.

But i must not brood. The path of memory is neither straight nor safe, and we travel down it at our own risk. It is easier to take short journeys into the past, remembering in miniature, constructing tiny puppet plays in our heads.

Each image carries with it a sense of loss, even if the loss is tinged, no matter how faintly, with relief. Age carries strange burdens with it, and one of them, perhaps inevitably, is death.

That's the way to do it.

My great-uncle Morton was always my favourite adult relative. Not because he was any more or less pleasant to me than any other – indeed i do not remember any particular acts of kindness, except for a half-crown bribe, which i shall come to later – but because Morton was the first adult i was able to look in the eye.

Lacking a photograph, i try to form his face in my mind. Hair dark as mine, a jagged brow and a crooked grin and between them a proud Jewish nose, hooked and jutting. Above the nose two bright grey eyes.

And strong as his face i recall his back.

Morton was a hunchback; small and smart. By the time i was eight i was as tall as he, and that was so good.

He was never part of my life, in the way that any of my grandparents were.

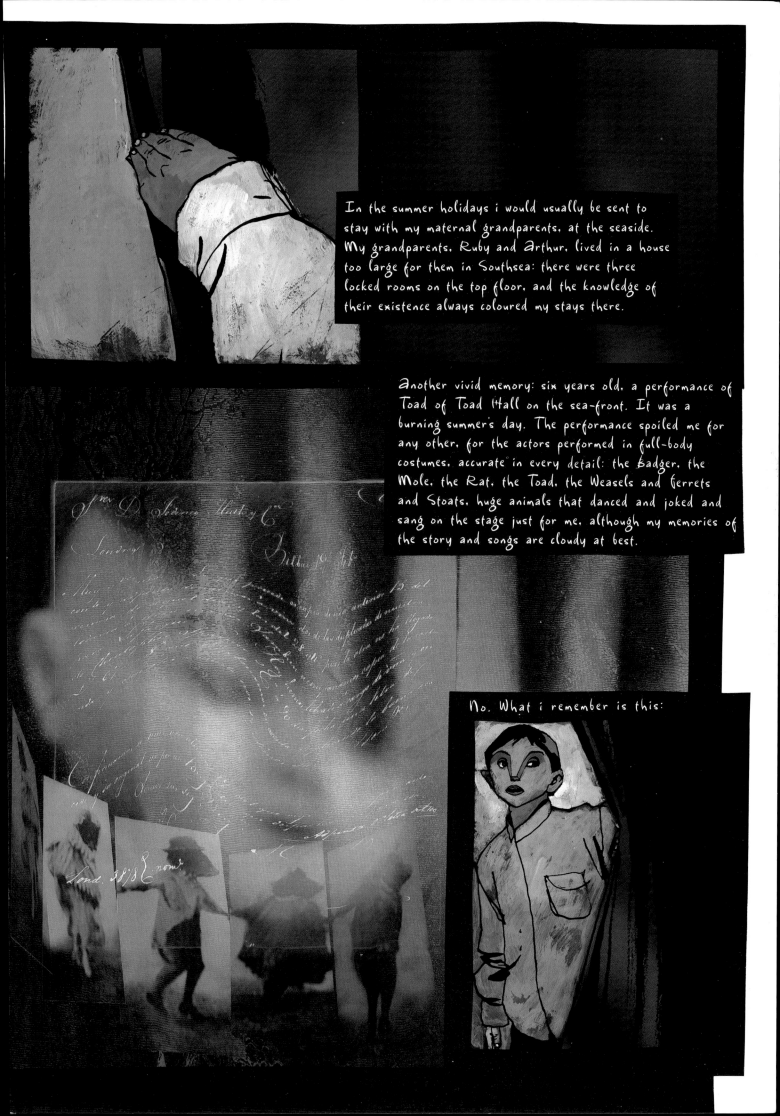

In the summer holidays i would usually be sent to stay with my maternal grandparents, at the seaside. My grandparents, Ruby and Arthur, lived in a house too large for them in Southsea: there were three locked rooms on the top floor, and the knowledge of their existence always coloured my stays there.

Another vivid memory: six years old, a performance of Toad of Toad Hall on the sea-front. It was a burning summer's day. The performance spoiled me for any other, for the actors performed in full-body costumes, accurate in every detail: the Badger, the Mole, the Rat, the Toad, the Weasels and ferrets and Stoats, huge animals that danced and joked and sang on the stage just for me, although my memories of the story and songs are cloudy at best.

No. What i remember is this:

After the performance was over i passed backstage — an open-air pavilion —

and saw the animals unfastening their heads, removing their skins; pink, sweating humans climbing out of the animal costumes, calling to each other, talking.

The badger's empty head lay on a chair, dead and silent.

I knelt and touched it.

I waited for it to whisper secrets to me, but it said nothing.

and my grandmother took my hand and pulled me away.

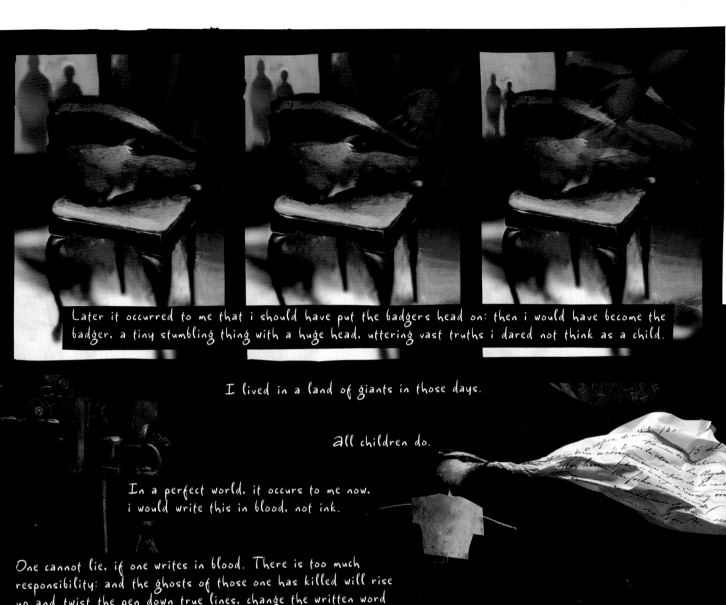

Later it occurred to me that i should have put the badger's head on: then i would have become the badger. a tiny stumbling thing with a huge head. uttering vast truths i dared not think as a child.

I lived in a land of giants in those days.

all children do.

In a perfect world. it occurs to me now.
i would write this in blood. not ink.

One cannot lie. if one writes in blood. There is too much responsibility: and the ghosts of those one has killed will rise up and twist the pen down true lines. change the written word to the unwritten as the red lines fade on the page to brown.

That's why deals with the Devil must be signed in blood. If you sign your name in blood. it's your real name. You can't change it.

There. now. And already I'm speaking of blood:
and it's the past i meant to speak of.

And the dead. of course. there's no getting away from the dead.

"Punch and Judy men die in the gutter." That was what Mister Swatchell. the Punch and Judy man. told me. when i was a boy. "We die in the gutter. or the workhouse, or we don't die at all. There's never any getting away from that."

That was a year later. of course. when i was eight.

My mother was very pregnant. and i had been sent away for three weeks. to stay with my father's parents. I didn't know why.

Much later it was explained to me that i had just had one of the routine childhood diseases - chicken pox. or mumps. or possibly German Measles - and it was thought that i might infect my mother. or my soon-to-be-born baby sister.

In later years my other sister was to crow about this. "I saw her first" she'd say. "That's why she's my friend best. You weren't even here when she was born."

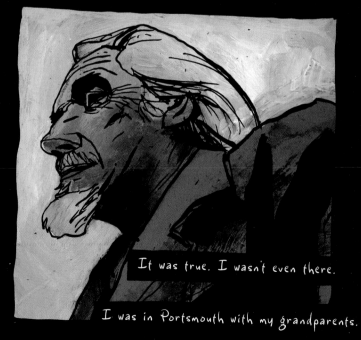

It was true. I wasn't even there.

I was in Portsmouth with my grandparents.

This was shortly before my grandfather went mad.

He had a huge black Daimler, which he eventually crashed into a wall. He walked away, physically unharmed, but he was never the same.

All his affairs, business and otherwise, were over, and he stayed at home all day, shouting at my grandmother, spitting saliva in his fury of words.

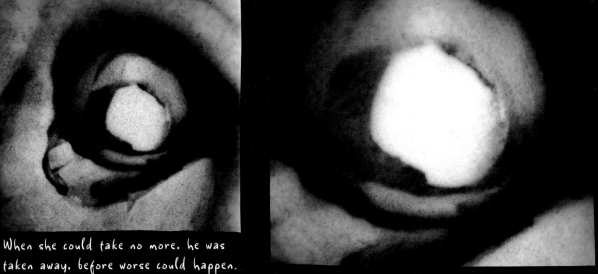

When she could take no more, he was taken away, before worse could happen.

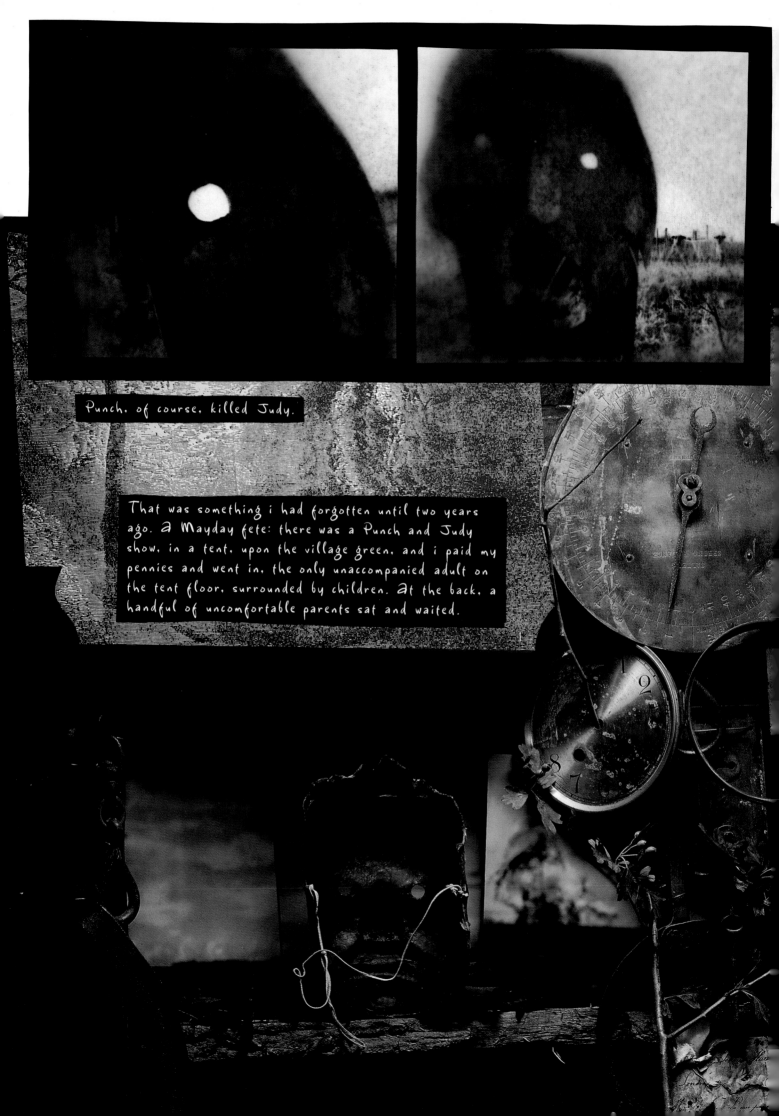

Punch, of course, killed Judy.

That was something i had forgotten until two years ago. a Mayday fete: there was a Punch and Judy show, in a tent, upon the village green, and i paid my pennies and went in, the only unaccompanied adult on the tent floor, surrounded by children. at the back, a handful of uncomfortable parents sat and waited.

I had heard that they had sweetened the show in recent years, extracted all murder and hurt and revenge from it. But no, after Punch had killed the baby, Judy returned and asked him where it was.

What baby?

The baby - our baby, you wicked old man. I left it with you to mind, didn't i boys and girls?

It's asleep.

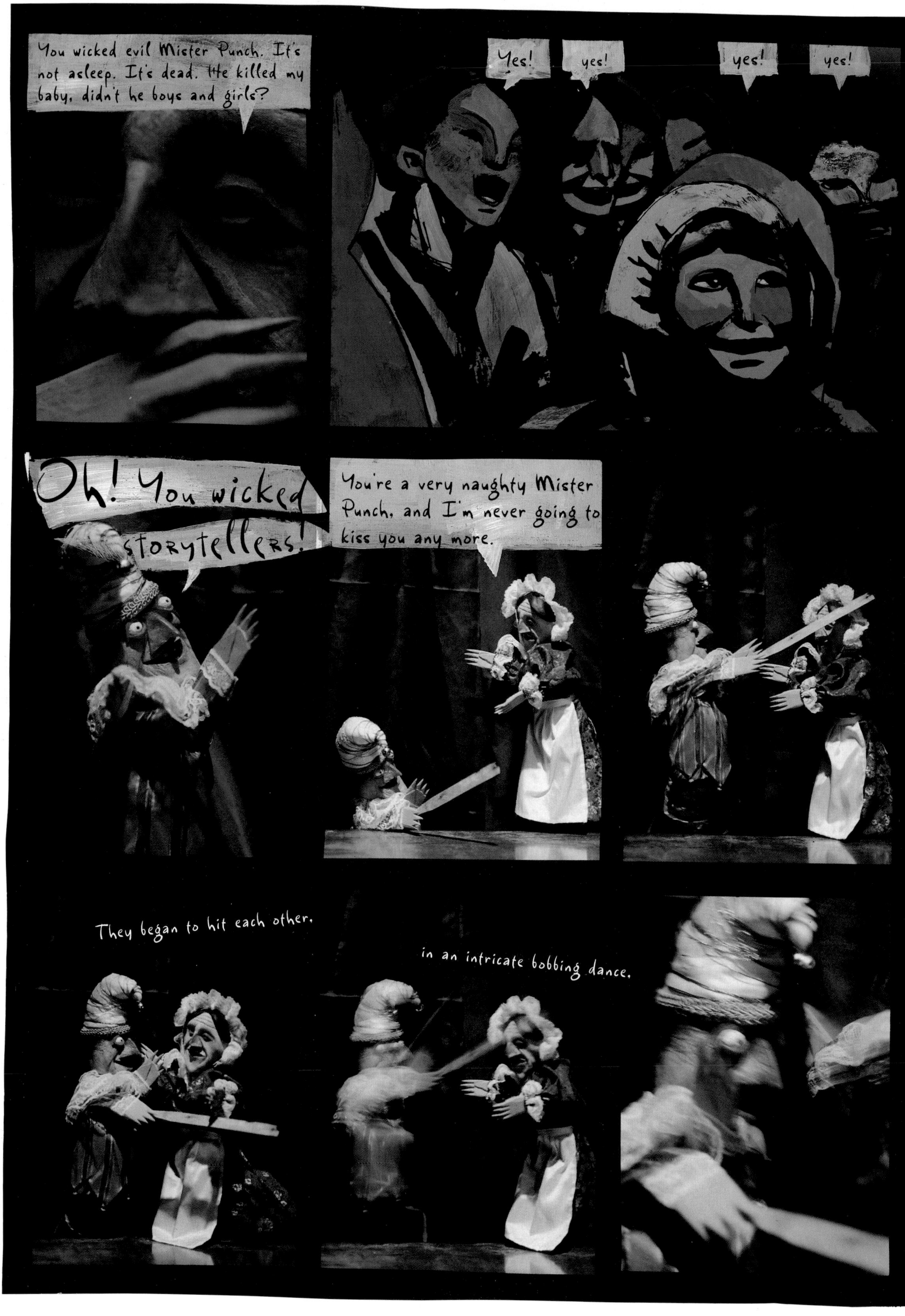
You wicked evil Mister Punch. It's not asleep. It's dead. He killed my baby, didn't he boys and girls?
Yes!
yes!
yes!
yes!
Oh! You wicked storytellers!
You're a very naughty Mister Punch, and I'm never going to kiss you any more.
They began to hit each other,
in an intricate bobbing dance.

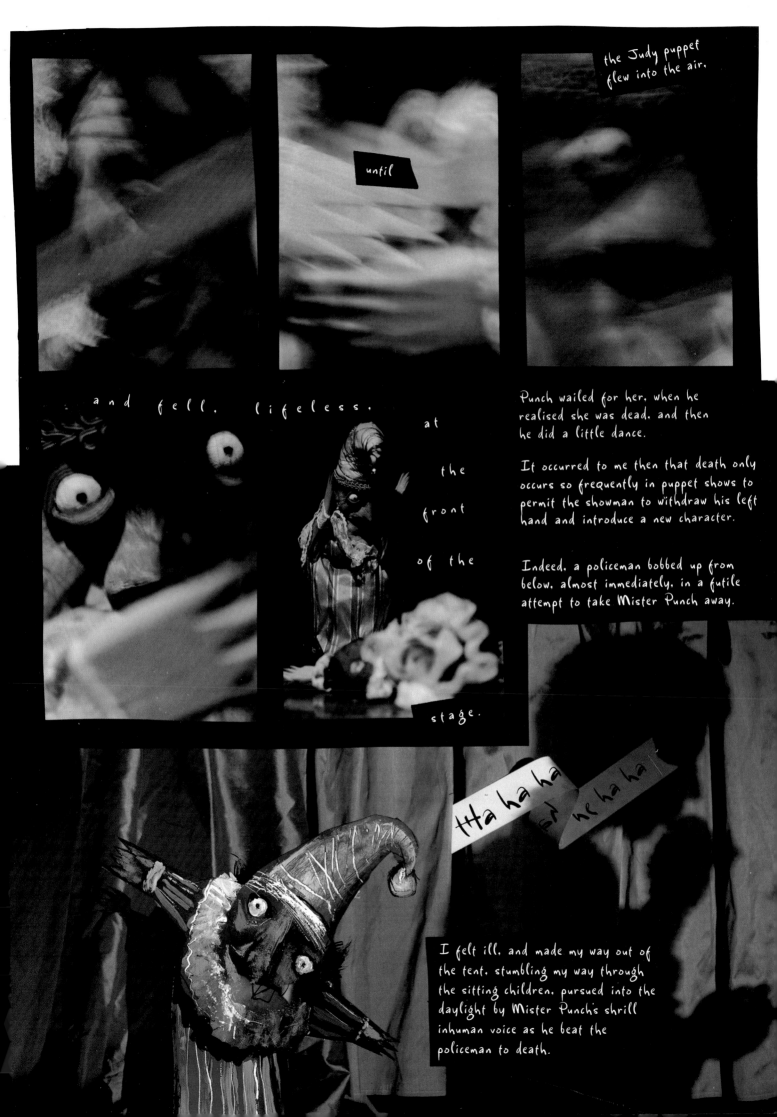

the Judy puppet flew into the air,

until

and fell, lifeless,

at

the

front

of the

stage.

Punch wailed for her, when he realised she was dead, and then he did a little dance.

It occurred to me then that death only occurs so frequently in puppet shows to permit the showman to withdraw his left hand and introduce a new character.

Indeed, a policeman bobbed up from below, almost immediately, in a futile attempt to take Mister Punch away.

Ha ha ha he ha ha

I felt ill, and made my way out of the tent, stumbling my way through the sitting children, pursued into the daylight by Mister Punch's shrill inhuman voice as he beat the policeman to death.

I remember playing card games with my grandfather. Games of memory, not of skill. If i won, he gave me sixpence; if he won, he didn't. We would play until i was bored, or until he ran out of sixpences.

He had sold his grocery chain, and now only had a small amusement arcade on the sea-front.

No, I'm being imprecise. It wasn't on the sea-front. It was just far enough away from the sea-front to be a complete commercial failure. At some time in the past it might have been a warehouse. i suppose, or an aircraft hangar. My grandfather had bought it cheaply and turned it into an inferior copy of the local pier.

It was a half-empty maze of old slot machines. of shops and booths. There was a mirror maze; an elderly woman in a headscarf who sat beneath a sign with a human palm on it and drank tea from a thermos flask; a small menagerie of huge. wicked-looking parrots. angry reds and vivid blues. that squawked in high. unintelligible voices;

and, at the top of the building, on a rock, in the middle of a very small artificial lake, there was a mermaid.

To get to the mermaid you had to walk up the narrow path, past the hall of mirrors, past the entrance to the ghost train, past the ice-cream concession and the little shop that sold the saucy postcards.

If i close my eyes and remember, i can still hear the mermaid singing, in her high, reedy voice. She only had one song.

People would stare at her.

I wonder
f one day that
you'd say that
you care
madly

The lake - in actuality a large glass tank - had transparent sides, thick with green algae, and a rock sticking out of the water, and on the top of the rock the mermaid sat, combing out her hair, and singing.

She would pick up her comb, and pretend to comb out her very long wet blonde wig, and mutter something about this one coming from sandy shores, then sing:

"I wonder if one day-that you say-that you care

If you say you love me-madly I'll gladly be there..."

You didn't have to pay anything to see the mermaid. She was an attraction.

You can't stop things from changing.

that's my grandfather talking. in my head. h voice cigarette-roughened. street-smart. with pride of a man who has dragged himself up from street level and now drives a Daimler.

You've seen the receipts. They're staying away in bloody droves.

I'm ahead of my time. That's all. I'm ahead of my time.

They stood watching the mermaid. two men in expensive coats. both chain-smoking Peter Stuyvesants. one taller than me. one my height. and i stood with them. small. licking my ice cream.

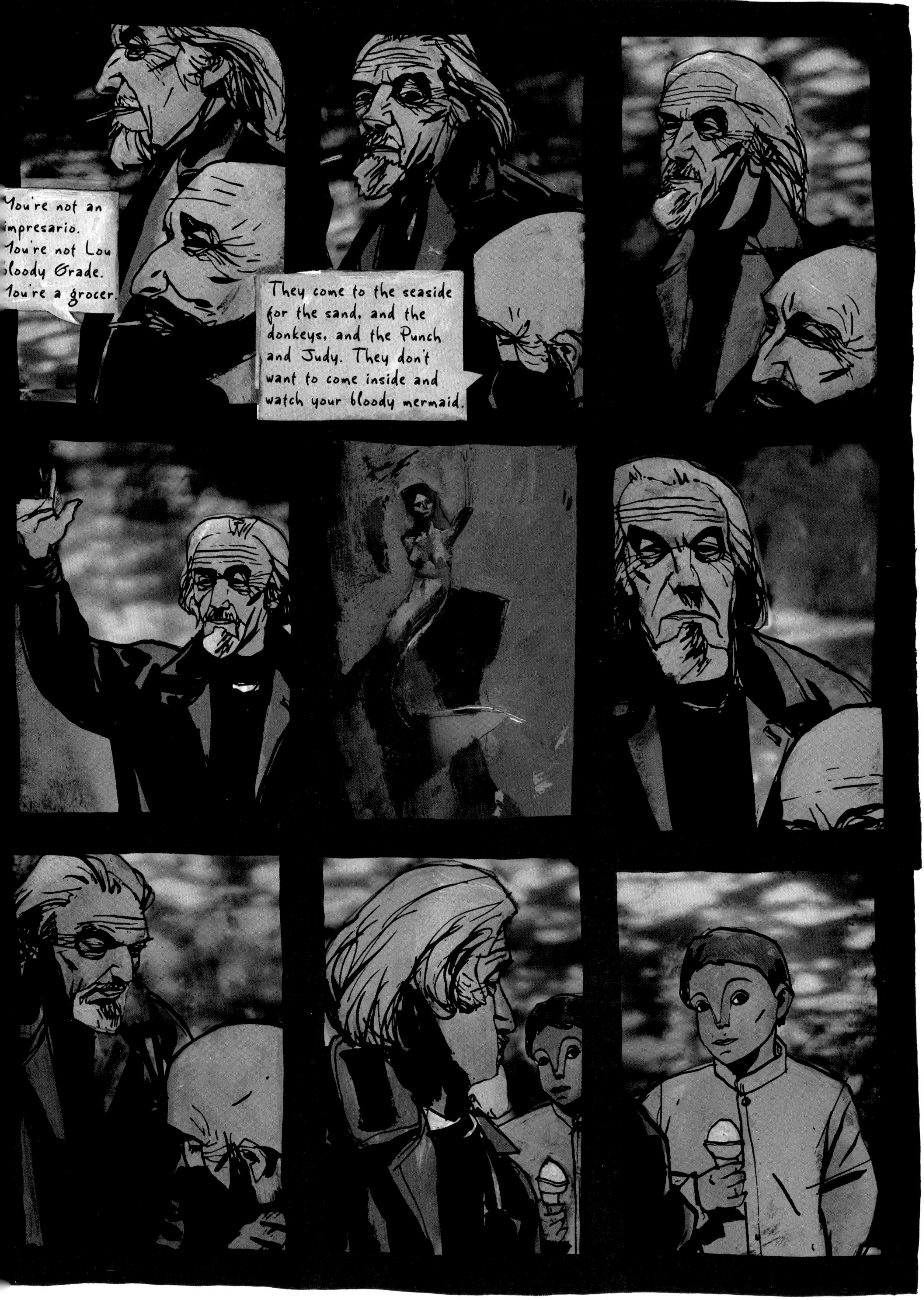
You're not an impresario. You're not Lou bloody Grade. You're a grocer.
They come to the seaside for the sand, and the donkeys, and the Punch and Judy. They don't want to come inside and watch your bloody mermaid.

My grandfather picked me up.

Shall i throw you in, eh? Shall i throw you in the water?

I shook my head.

Adults are threatening creatures.

Shall i throw you in the water?

I'll put you into the rubbish-bin.

I'll eat you all up.

That's what they say. And no matter how much you tell yourself that they're lying, or teasing, there's always a chance. Maybe they are telling the truth.

I'll take you back and get another little boy.

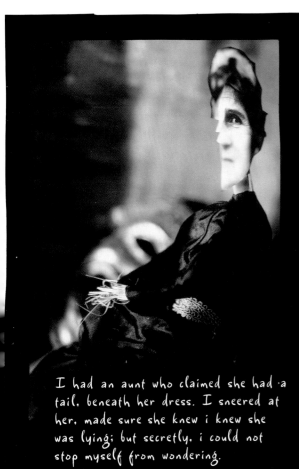

I had an aunt who claimed she had a tail, beneath her dress. I sneered at her, made sure she knew i knew she was lying; but secretly, i could not stop myself from wondering.

Adults lie.

but not always.

When i was four i believed everything. accepted everything. and was scared of nothing. Now i was eight. and i believed in what i could see and was scared of anything i couldn't. Scared of things in the darkness. of things invisible to see.

My grandfather put me down. I was too heavy for him to carry. now.

We walked over to the nearest point to the mermaid's rock. and my grandfather leaned over.

He smiled at her.

...How's it going?

Mustn't grumble.

There's a girl. You come down to the office later, we'll reckon up.

We walked back through the arcade.

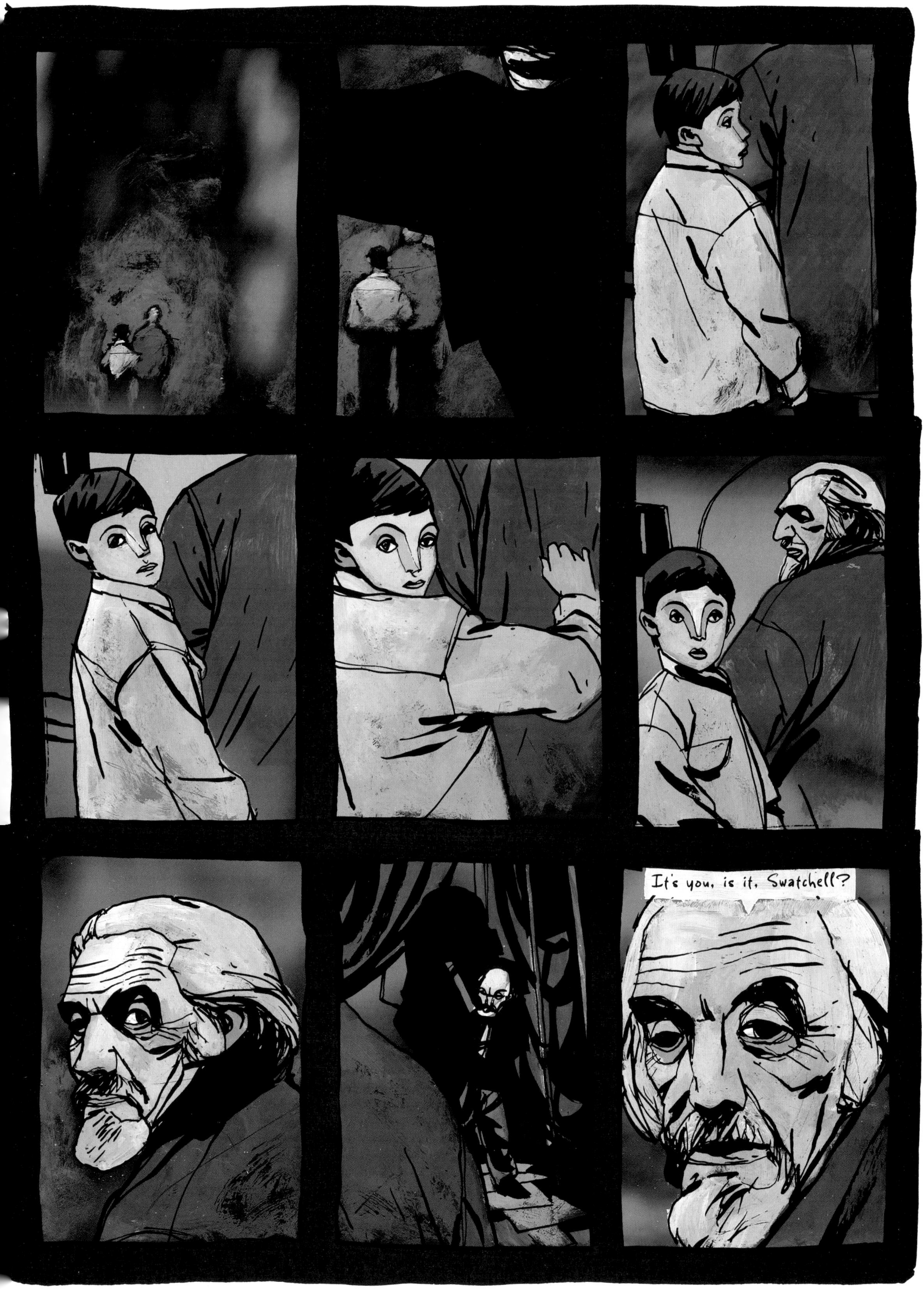
It's you, is it, Swatchell?

It's me.

Never thought I'd see you again. What do you want, then?

And is that any way to say hello to an old friend?

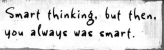

It's a good place you got here.

When it rains, they won't go away. Indeed, when it rains they'll come in here.

Smart thinking, but then, you always was smart.

Except for that time in Wales, with the soap. Remember that?

What do you want?

This must be your grandson. Come here lad, and say hello to my little Toby dog. There's few enough of the professors have dogs any more, and never a one of them can perform like our Toby.

Hut and over boy.

Swatchell. What do you want?

I want to pitch here.

You must be out of your mind. If you think I'm letting you put up your show in my arcade...

Now, before you say anything you'll regret, we should talk about this.

They walked off together, leaving me alone with my uncle Morton and the Toby dog.

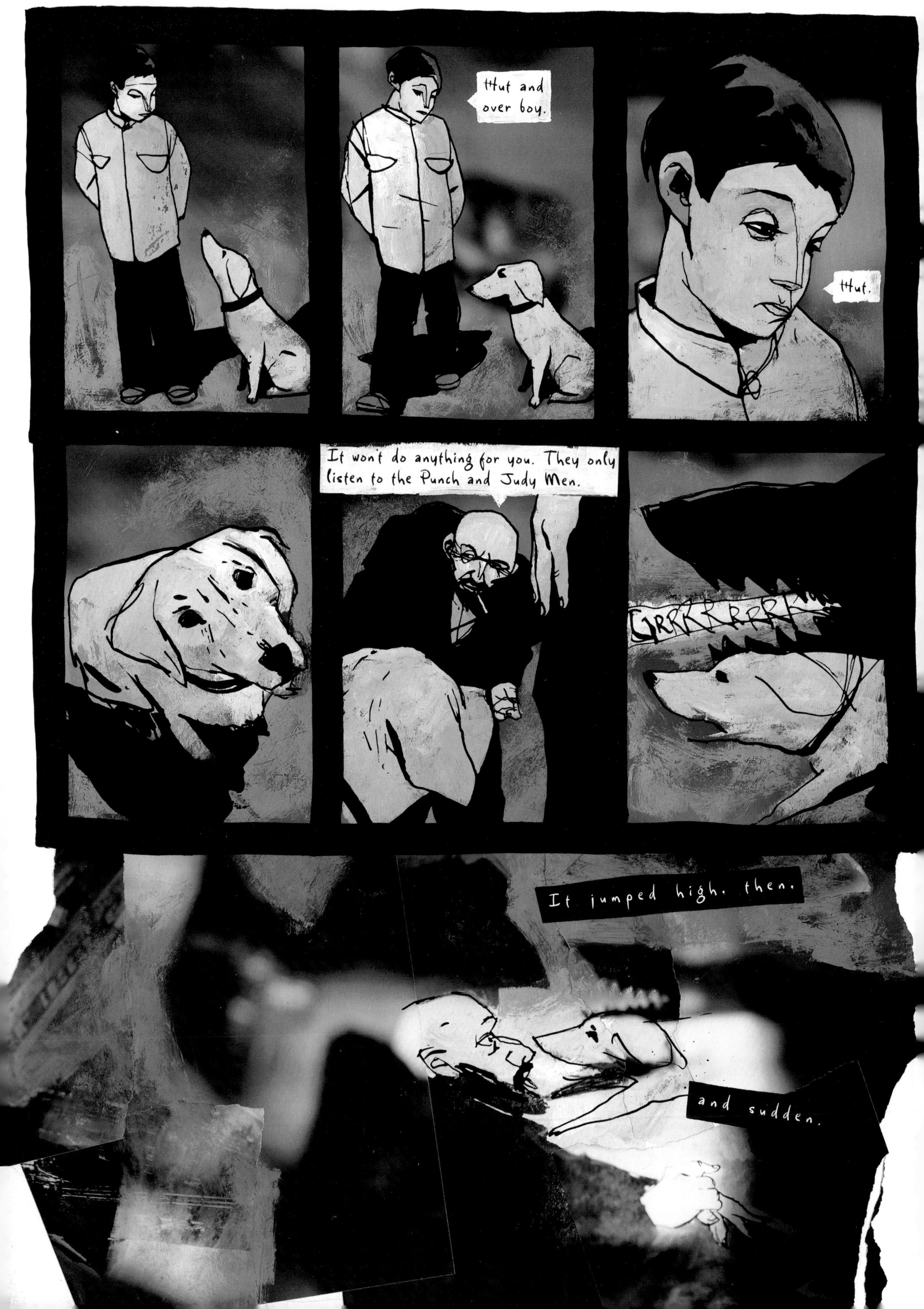
Hut and over boy.
Hut.
It won't do anything for you. They only listen to the Punch and Judy Men.
GRRRRRRRR
It jumped high, then,
and sudden.

Jumped at my uncle.

Bad dog.
Bad bad
dog..

Well?

He can set up here, by the door.

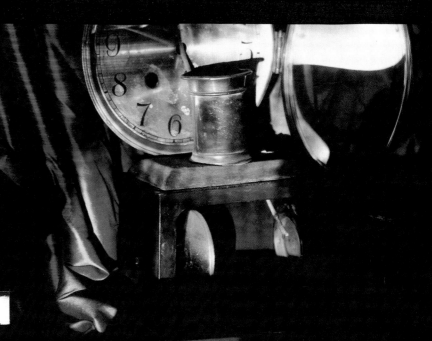

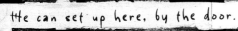

Next Performance

first performance, four o'clock.

Where's your bottler, then?

Two years inside. Breaking and entering. Pity. I'd always found him to be unutterable honest.

Still, people, eh? Mystery plays the lot of them.

Hey, boy. are you honest?

I don't know. Sometimes.

Maybe you could be my bottler, hey?

But he laughed when he said it. in the way adults do. to show you that they don't mean what they're saying.

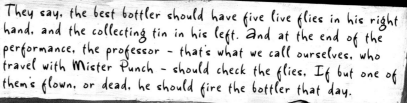

They say, the best bottler should have five live flies in his right hand. and the collecting tin in his left. And at the end of the performance, the professor - that's what we call ourselves, who travel with Mister Punch - should check the flies. If but one of them's flown, or dead, he should fire the bottler that day.

He told me. Every Punch and Judy professor has a bottler - the person whose task it is to take round the collecting tin for the Punch and Judy show.

A good bottler, said Mister Swatchell, did more than that, though. A bottler starts the backchat with the puppets from the audience. A bottler makes sure that no children are sneaking round the back of the booth, that no dogs raise their legs against the side of it. If a policeman comes to move you on, the bottler'll make sure you finish the show first. Some bottlers even blow trumpets...

They all laughed at that.

Then my grandfather put me in his car and drove me back to his house. I don't know where my Uncle Morton went. If he had a house I'd never been there.

I asked my grandfather what the man had meant, about the soap in Wales. He said i should mind my own business; that if i asked no questions i would be told no lies. I wanted to ask whether, if i asked many questions, i would be told many lies, but i held my tongue. Adults do what adults do: they live in a bigger world to which children are denied access.

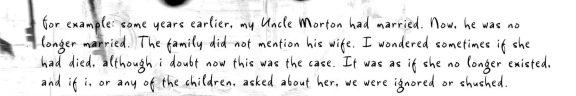

For example: some years earlier, my Uncle Morton had married. Now, he was no longer married. The family did not mention his wife. I wondered sometimes if she had died, although i doubt now this was the case. It was as if she no longer existed, and if i, or any of the children, asked about her, we were ignored or shushed.

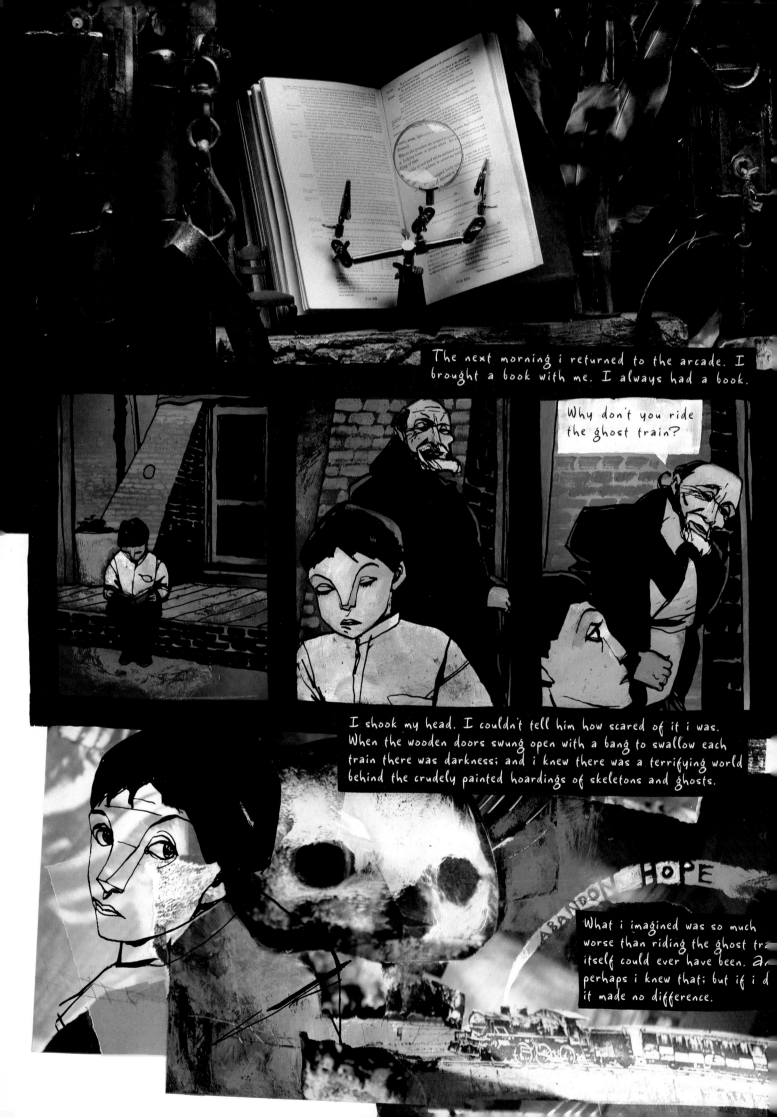

The next morning i returned to the arcade. I brought a book with me. I always had a book.

Why don't you ride the ghost train?

I shook my head. I couldn't tell him how scared of it i was. When the wooden doors swung open with a bang to swallow each train there was darkness; and i knew there was a terrifying world behind the crudely painted hoardings of skeletons and ghosts.

ABANDON HOPE

What i imagined was so much worse than riding the ghost train itself could ever have been. and perhaps i knew that; but if i did it made no difference.

Well, you won't get another chance. They'll be out of here tomorrow. Off to somewhere where the punters are.

Do you want to see the cast?

Who?

The cast of the play

the greatest, oldest, wisest play there is: the comical tragedy, the tragical comedy, of Mister Punch.

Yes, please.

Come on, then.

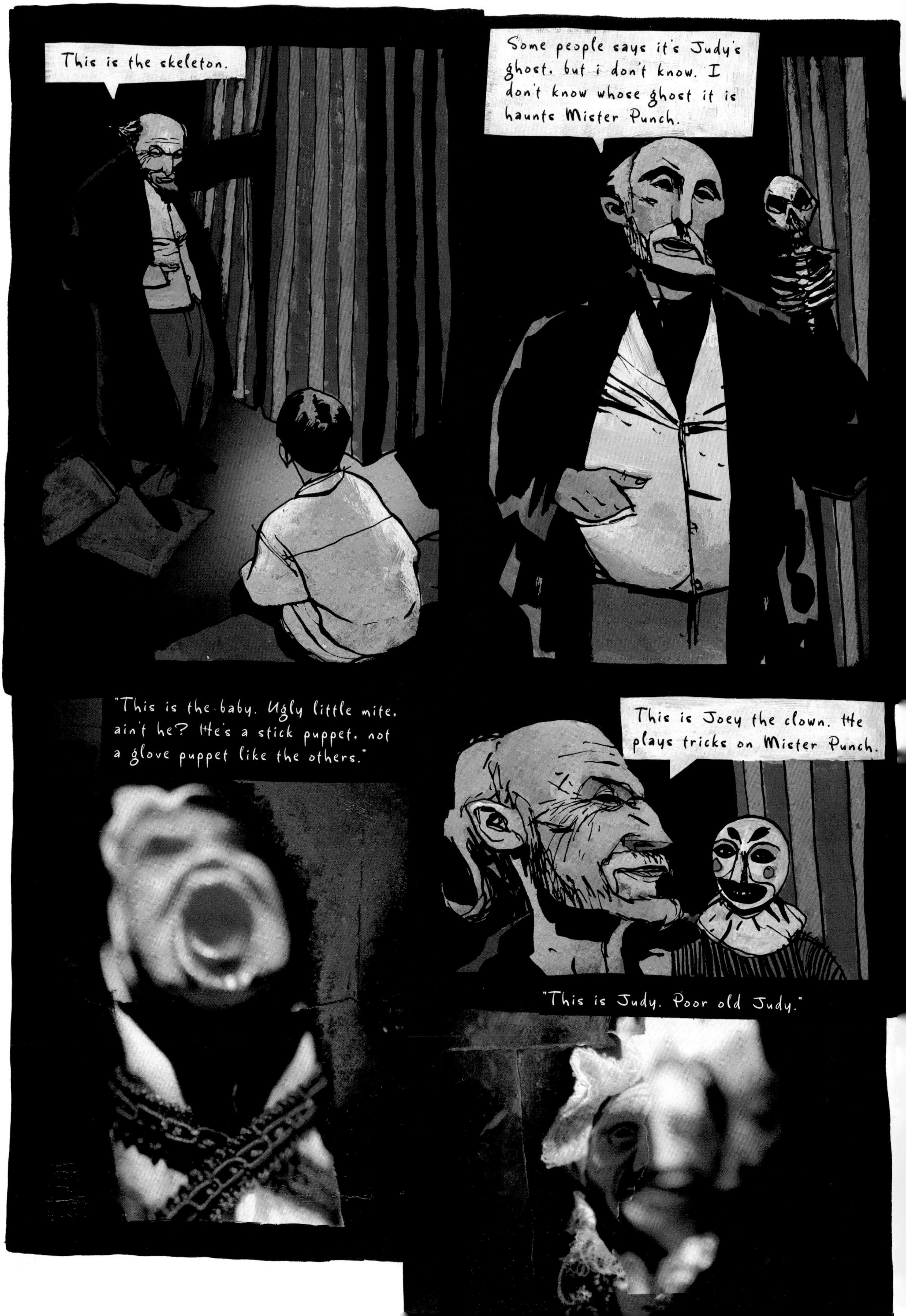
This is the skeleton.
Some people says it's Judy's ghost, but i don't know. I don't know whose ghost it is haunts Mister Punch.
"This is the baby. Ugly little mite, ain't he? He's a stick puppet, not a glove puppet like the others."
This is Joey the clown. He plays tricks on Mister Punch.
"This is Judy. Poor old Judy."

"This is the doctor. He finds Mister Punch laying on the ground. 'Are ye dead?' says he. 'Stone cold dead.' says Mister Punch, but he's lying a-course. 'I'll give you physic.' says the doctor - that's medicine. the way we used to call it in the dawn days. And he comes back with his stick. Physic, physic, physic.

"This is the Devil. He comes on at the end. to drag Mister Punch away to hell. I remember some busybodies. in the last queen's day, telling me that he ought to succeed. But he never does, there's always a Devil in the story of Mister Punch, although sometimes he's hard to find."

This is the beadle - the blackbeetle, as Mister Punch calls him. He tries to hang Mister Punch, but Mister Punch is too clever for him.

Now, here are the old members of the cast who no longer have a part in the tragedy. This is Pretty Polly - she's Mister Punch's little bit of stuff, heh? Mister Punch's girlfriend.

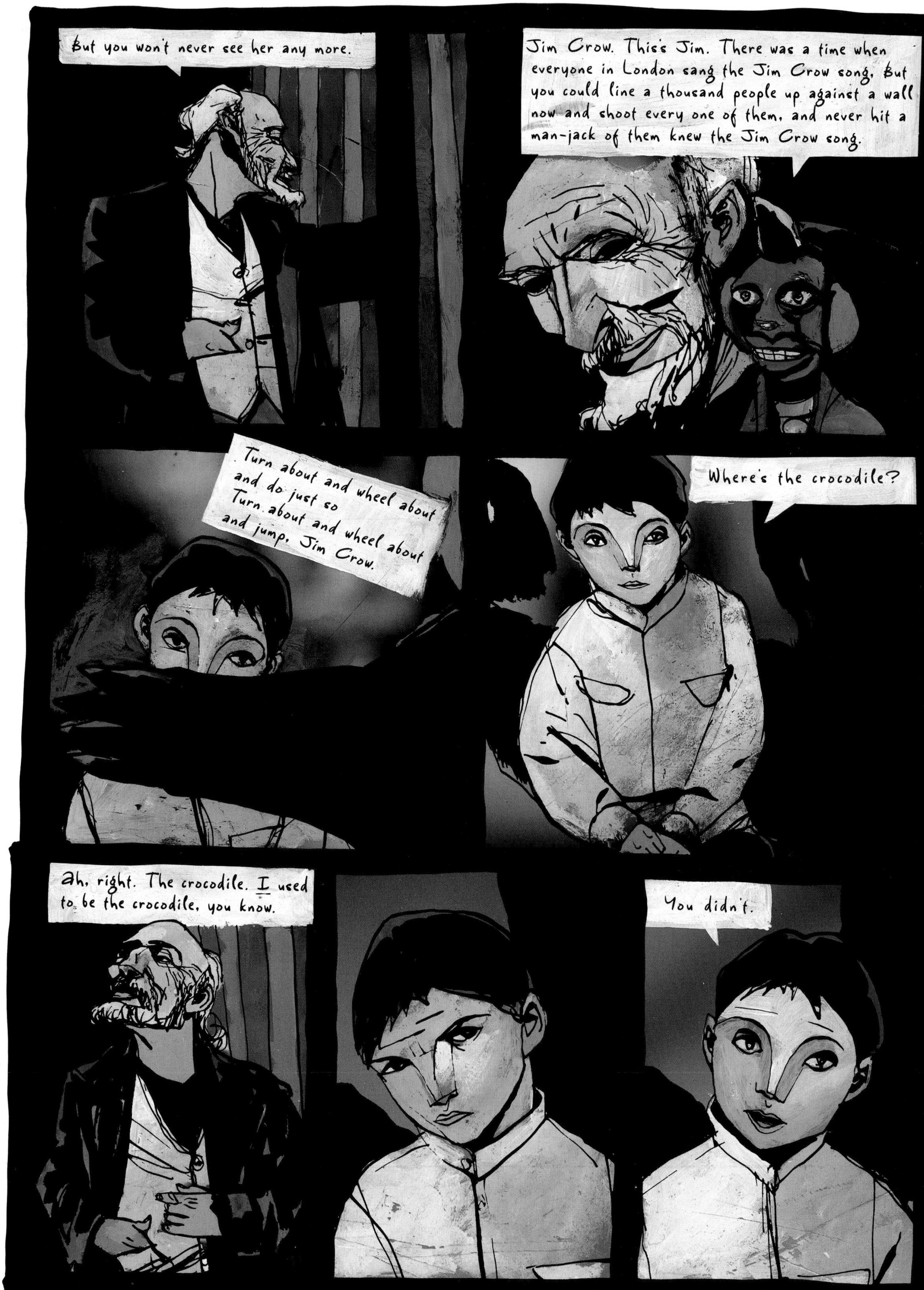
But you won't never see her any more.
Jim Crow. This's Jim. There was a time when everyone in London sang the Jim Crow song, but you could line a thousand people up against a wall now and shoot every one of them, and never hit a man-jack of them knew the Jim Crow song.
Turn about and wheel about and do just so Turn about and wheel about and jump, Jim Crow.
Where's the crocodile?
Ah, right. The crocodile. I used to be the crocodile, you know.
You didn't.

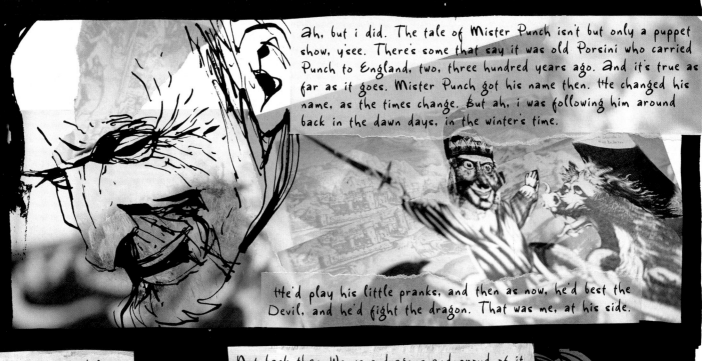

ah, but i did. The tale of Mister Punch isn't but only a puppet show, y'see. There's some that say it was old Porsini who carried Punch to England, two, three hundred years ago. And it's true as far as it goes. Mister Punch got his name then. He changed his name, as the times change. But ah, i was following him around back in the dawn days, in the winter's time.

He'd play his little pranks, and then as now, he'd best the Devil, and he'd fight the dragon. That was me, at his side.

Not a crocodile?

Not back then. We were dragons and proud of it.

The crocodile writhed greenly on his arm, grinning up at us with sharp white teeth.

Can i try it?

He pulled the crocodile off his arm.

It hung, empty and dead, like a sock. I took it, warily.

On the left hand. It's only Mister Punch himself goes on your right hand. He goes on, and he stays on.

Later i observed this to be true: Punch dominates the left side of the stage; and in this there is nothing sinister. He is a right hand puppet. and he stays on all the time: the others – the ghosts and clowns and women and devils, they come on and they go off.

Mister Punch never goes away.

I slid the puppet onto my left hand:

and it came to life.

I'm not talking about anything fantastical here. You can try it yourself – find a hand-puppet, slide it on your arm. flex your hand, move your fingers. And somehow, in the cold space between one moment and the next, the puppet becomes alive.

And the crocodile was alive.

I didn't ever want to give it back. I wanted it to sit on my arm forever, brave where i was fearful, impetuous where i held back. I would have taken it to school and scared my teachers, taken it home and made it eat my sister...

The Punch and Judy man held out his hand.

Reluctantly, i pulled off the crocodile and gave it back to him. He hung it inside the theatre, from a brass hook.

Where's Punch?

Mister Punch is resting before his next performance.

Can i try him on?

Once you bring Mister Punch to life, there's no getting rid of him. But you can watch the show. You'll see him then.

How do you make him do the voice?

He shook his head, slowly.

Everybody's got secrets, boy. And Mister Punch's voice is one of mine..

I'm taking Toby Dog here for a walk, before the next show. After all, he's got to do his business somewhere, eh?

Hut and over boy.

ater forms has continued t
' forms of mask and pupp
erged in the practices of
acceptable definitions of
evitably remain fixed on
life a play text on a stag
er, which in the west had
allenged for over three
by various theater artis
of the last century, when
actors on realistic stag
ly adequa
ern society.

I sat on the hamper and read my book.

My grandfather was in the arcade office with a man from the bank.

The Punch and Judy man came back with his new bottler.

His bottler was a thin man, with greasy black hair. His face had red splotchy pimples all over it.

It has now occurred to me that the bottler, whose name I've forgotten if i ever knew it, was probably only fifteen or sixteen: and all this time i had thought of him - when I've thought of him, which was seldom - as an adult, when he was little more than a boy.

I got off the hamper and went round to the front.

Punch:

There were a few other kids there, already, waiting. Toby Dog sat on the stage with a ruff around his neck and barked; but no-one else came.

When Punch came on, the Toby dog bit him on the nose.

A skeleton came out, behind him, onto the stage. It was a ghost.

Punch killed the baby, and Judy. Then he killed the policeman who came to take him away.

Punch didn't see it.

They bobbed around the stage until Punch finally caught sight of the ghost, and was frightened.

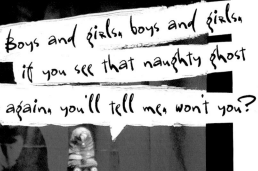

Boys and girls, boys and girls, if you see that naughty ghost again, you'll tell me, won't you?

Of course they will, won't you boys and girls?

Come on you lot. Let's hear you shout for Mister Punch.

I can't hear you.

None of us said anything. We wouldn't. Not even me.

The ghost jiggled up behind Punch. and the bottler shouted:

It's behind you!

Punch turned. but the ghost had ducked away.

The ghost bounced up again. It ma[de] its neck stretch until i thought its head would come off [wh]en Mister Punch hit it and ma[de it] go away.

"That's the way to do it."

said Mister Punch. in his high tinny voice.

He said it all as one word:

"at'sawaytodoit!"

The little girl sitting next to me burst into tears. H[er] mother. who was standing near. came over and took her away.

The show continued. all i remember was hoping that someone would finally kill the nasty little red man. with his squeaking voice and his banging stick.

Many tried - the doctor. and the crocodile. the hangman and the Devil - but each one failed.

And at the end, he waved his stick at us.

Bye-bye boys and girls.

Bye bye.

I waved back, although i knew it was just a puppet, and it scared me.

. The little curtains closed.

Swatchell came out, and set the "Next performance" clock for half an hour's time.

The bottler gave him the handful of pennies he'd collected. One of them was mine.

There was a storm that night; lightning made the night sky flicker and flare.

I watched the storm from my darkened bedroom in my grandparents' house, staring as the landscape outside the window appeared and vanished into blackness. fractional and colourless, like the past. I rejoiced in the dark rolling booms of the thunder, and counted the interval between the blaze and the boom, and listened to the beat of the rain on the window, and was glad that i was safe and warm.

Eventually i slept. and i
dreamed a dream

I was back in the arcade, and it was
after dark. There were shadows
everywhere. At first i wasn't scared.

I was following a path, lit by small
candles, through the darkness.
There was no-one there but me.

Then the rustlings began.

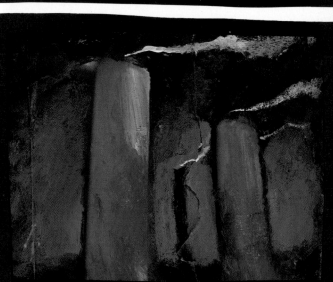

I heard the swish of their tails in the
darkness as they heard me coming, and
in the shadows they were smiling.

I knew what they were: Crocodiles and
alligators and older, huger reptiles, all with
teeth and eyes and scales and claws,
following me through the labyrinth of night.

One by one the candles
flickered and went out.

I began to run.

There was a light
ahead of me.

It came from the Punch
and Judy theatre.

On the stage the doctor was cutting open Pretty Polly.
Punch's forgotten girlfriend.

Punch stood beside him. looking sad.

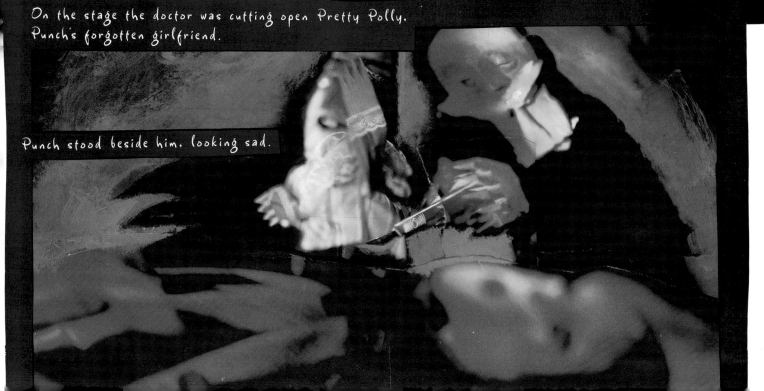

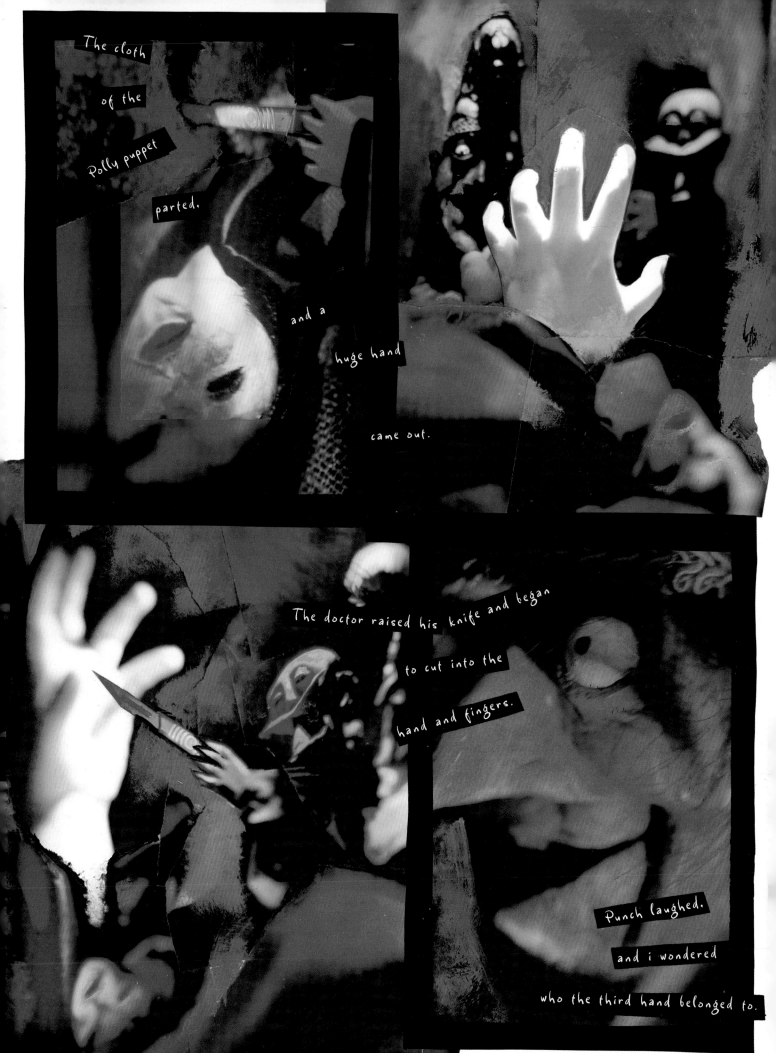

The cloth of the Polly puppet parted. and a huge hand came out.

The doctor raised his knife and began to cut into the hand and fingers.

Punch laughed. and i wondered who the third hand belonged to.

I turned to run: but there was nothing anywhere but the darkness.

No shelter.

no safety.

I had lost my way.

and i was alone

in the night.

And already the crocodiles were beginning to roar.

I woke in tears. to the roar of the thunder. and for one alien moment i was convinced that it was calling my name. The lightning illuminated the room. a flash so bright i could see colours.

I got out of bed and went into my grandmother's bedroom. She was sitting reading a romance novel, with her teeth out. My grandfather wasn't there. He had his own bedroom, which i had passed on the way through the darkened house: the door had been open, and a lightning flash had showed me that the bed was empty.

I got into bed with my grandmother, snuggled up against her massive reassuring bulk.

I never thought to ask where my grandfather was. You never think to ask questions like that, no more than it had ever occurred to me to wonder why they slept in separate rooms. He wasn't there and she was. That was just the way things were.

She turned out the light and went to sleep, and i lay in the darkness forever.

I woke back in my own room once more, and it was morning.

My grandfather always ate sausages for breakfast: a string of large kosher sausages, which my grandmother fried for him, and which sizzled and hissed in the pan, like live things.

That morning, however, my grandfather was not there. Perhaps he had never come home at all.

My parents telephoned. How was i? fine, i told them. fine. They seemed pleased.

The doctor would bring me a baby brother or sister very very soon, they told me. Maybe even tomorrow. What did i think of that?

It was okay, i said.

I wondered if my father would throw the baby out of the window: wondered whether it would break, if he did.

Why is Uncle Morton like he is? What happened to his back?

He was ill when he was a little baby. He had polio.

What's polio?

It's a disease.

Or T.B. I don't remember.

What's T.B.?

It's a disease.

My parents had given my grandparents a sum of money which they held for me in trust, to be disbursed in small increments each day. Today she gave me a shilling, and i walked down to the beach. It was a grey day, a chilly summer day that felt closer to winter than summer.

I walked along the seafront and wondered why the sea was painted blue in the books and pictures, when in real life it was a greenish-grey. The beach was almost deserted.

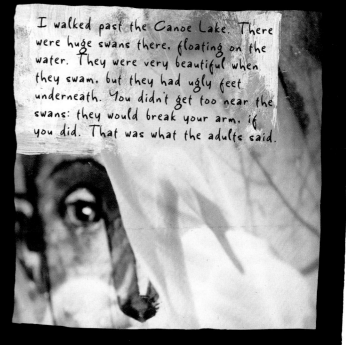

I walked past the Canoe Lake. There were huge swans there, floating on the water. They were very beautiful when they swam, but they had ugly feet underneath. You didn't get too near the swans: they would break your arm, if you did. That was what the adults said.

There was a Punch and Judy show set up beside the lake.
It was a poor thing, and shabby, and the show was already in progress.

Now, Mister Punch, you stay here and look after the sausages.

Oh. I've got sausages.

It's a pussy cat!

Pretty pussy.

Stroke the pretty pussy

Give me the sausages, pussy cat!

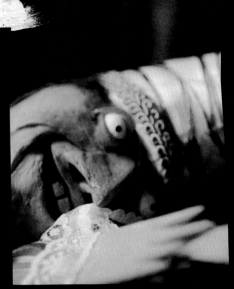

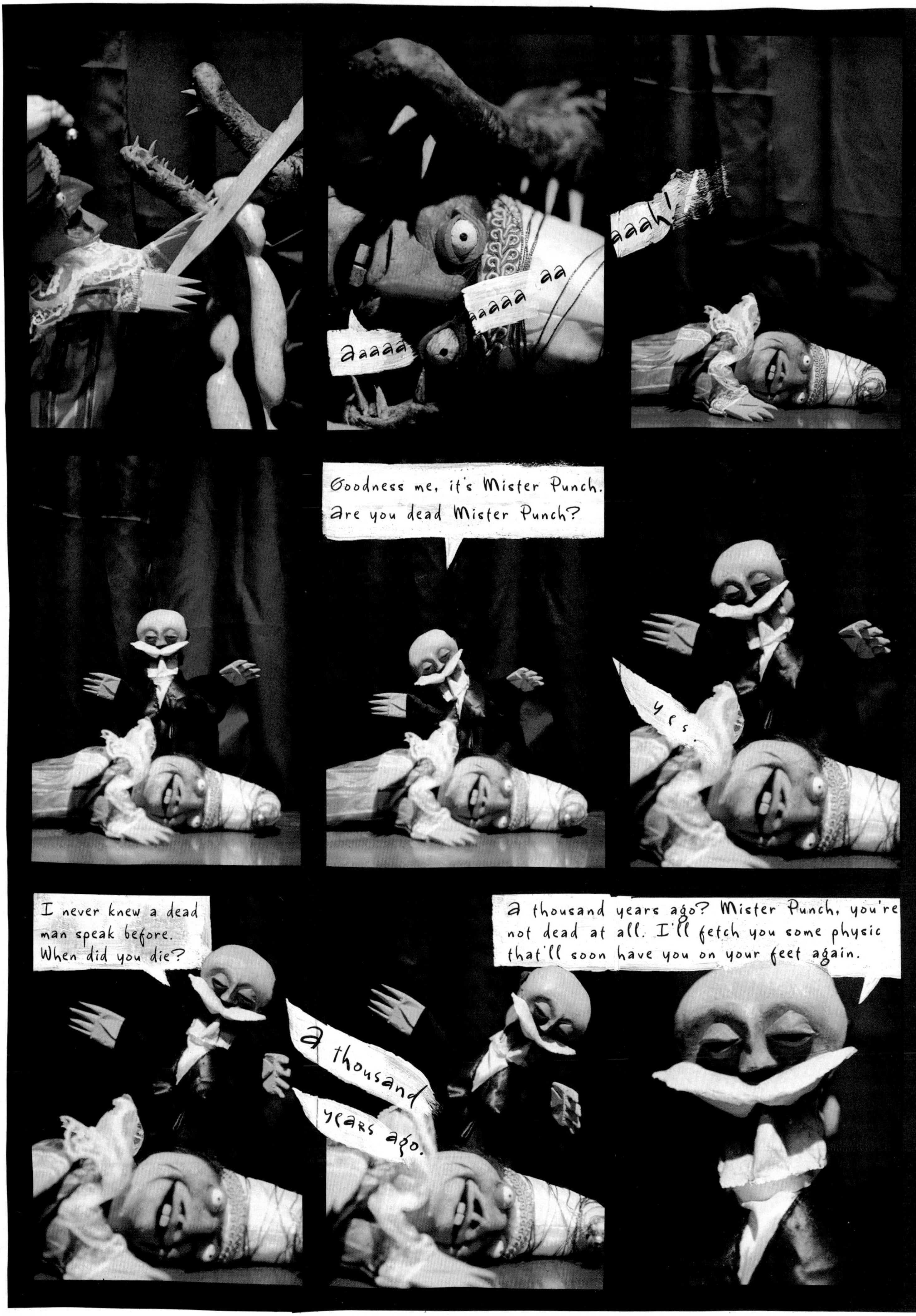
aaaaa
aaaaa aa
aaah!
Goodness me, it's Mister Punch. are you dead Mister Punch?
yes.
I never knew a dead man speak before. When did you die?
a thousand years ago.
a thousand years ago? Mister Punch, you're not dead at all. I'll fetch you some physic that'll soon have you on your feet again.

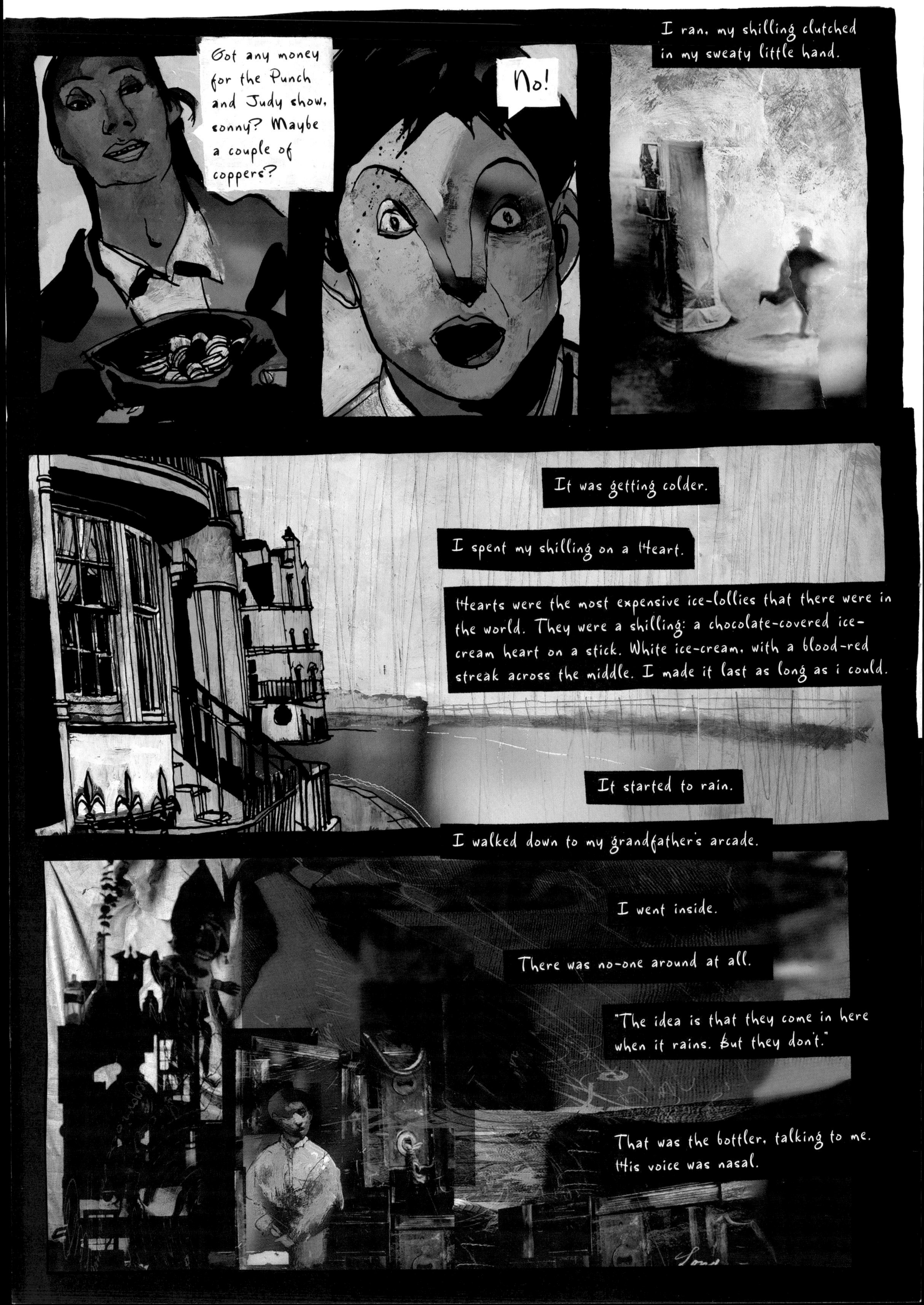
Got any money for the Punch and Judy show, sonny? Maybe a couple of coppers?
No!
I ran, my shilling clutched in my sweaty little hand.
It was getting colder.
I spent my shilling on a Heart.
Hearts were the most expensive ice-lollies that there were in the world. They were a shilling: a chocolate-covered ice-cream heart on a stick. White ice-cream, with a blood-red streak across the middle. I made it last as long as i could.
It started to rain.
I walked down to my grandfather's arcade.
I went inside.
There was no-one around at all.
"The idea is that they come in here when it rains. But they don't."
That was the bottler, talking to me. His voice was nasal.

Where's the Punch and Judy man?

Old Swatchell? I don't know. Maybe he's down at the pub. He's a bloody loony, if you ask me. Calling himself a professor, like anybody cares...

Punch and Judy. Who watches Punch and Judy? I tell you, ten years time, no-one'll remember it. Belongs in museums. This whole place belongs in a museum, you ask me.

Why?

There's telly now, isn't there? That's what people want. What i like are the police shows. In America they've got colour television. The pictures are all in colour.

You can see people talking and everything.

Is he your uncle or something?

The Punch and Judy man?

I just thought. I don't know. Something somebody said. I dunno.

You seen the mermaid recently? You ask me, she'll not be holding that job down much longer. Costume won't fit, for a start.

He laughed then, knowingly, and i laughed with him, flattered to feel included; although i had no idea to what he could be referring.

I walked up the ramp, past the place where huge, silent men were taking away the ghost train, packing up the plastic skeletons and the cardboard gravestones and the rubber masks, taking up the track and hauling down the little cars.

I walked past the hall of mirrors to the mermaid's lake.

a small hunchbacked man was talking to the mermaid, who was sitting on the rock.

I walked up close. They didn't see me coming. Perhaps she was getting fatter. It was hard to tell.

...after what bloody happened with the last one? Keeping that quiet was no picnic, believe you me.

Well, I'm not the last one, am i? and he loves me. He said so.

He's an old man. He doesn't love anybody.

Did he send you? Did he tell you to say this?

Nobody bloody sent me. It's just there's things that had to be said.

You're jealous. That's what you are. And you're nasty. And I'll tell you this for nothing, you little

Uh.

We've got company.

My uncle turned, and saw me, and smiled his crooked, friendly grin.

What are you doing up here, then?

I wanted to hear her singing.

Well, she's not singing right now. Here. Here's a half-crown. Go and have some fun with it. Don't spend it all in one place, eh? That's the way.

The mermaid had goose-bumps on her arms. She must have been very cold. I felt sorry for her.

That was the conversation as i recall it. I wish with all my heart, now, i could go back and talk to them, ask questions, illuminate the darkness of the past.

But these people are dead, and will not talk. Now that i want to go scrabbling around in the past, i cannot.

I was at a family wedding some months ago, and an aunt happened to mention my Great-Uncle Morton. I asked my question, then:

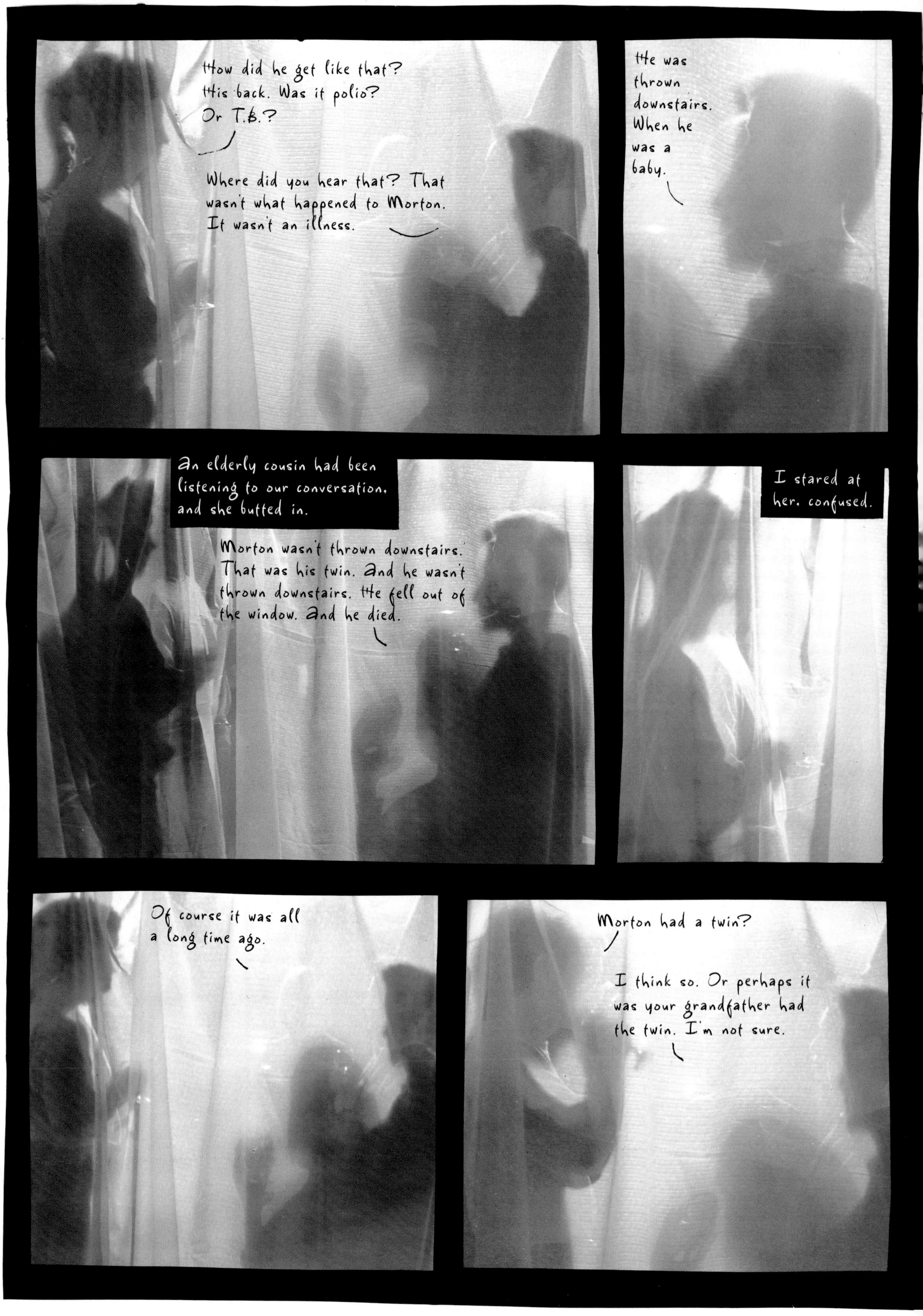
How did he get like that? His back. Was it polio? Or T.B.?
Where did you hear that? That wasn't what happened to Morton. It wasn't an illness.
He was thrown downstairs. When he was a baby.
An elderly cousin had been listening to our conversation, and she butted in.
Morton wasn't thrown downstairs. That was his twin. And he wasn't thrown downstairs. He fell out of the window. And he died.
I stared at her, confused.
Of course it was all a long time ago.
Morton had a twin?
I think so. Or perhaps it was your grandfather had the twin. I'm not sure.

With sixpence of my new-found half-crown i bought a comic from the mucky postcard shop. It was a black and white comic. cheaply reprinting older American tales. and was filled with short ghost stories: people who vanished or never existed. houses that weren't there the next time people went back to look for them. murdered wives who returned from the grave.

I spent the other two shillings on buying an entry ticket to the Hall of Mirrors. I'd always wanted to go in there.

To get in you had to walk through a maze constructed of mirrors and sheets of transparent glass. which went from floor to ceiling. You had to find your way through.

It would turn you around before you knew it. and several times i found myself lost within feet of the door that was my objective. The glass walls were highly polished. often quite invisible.

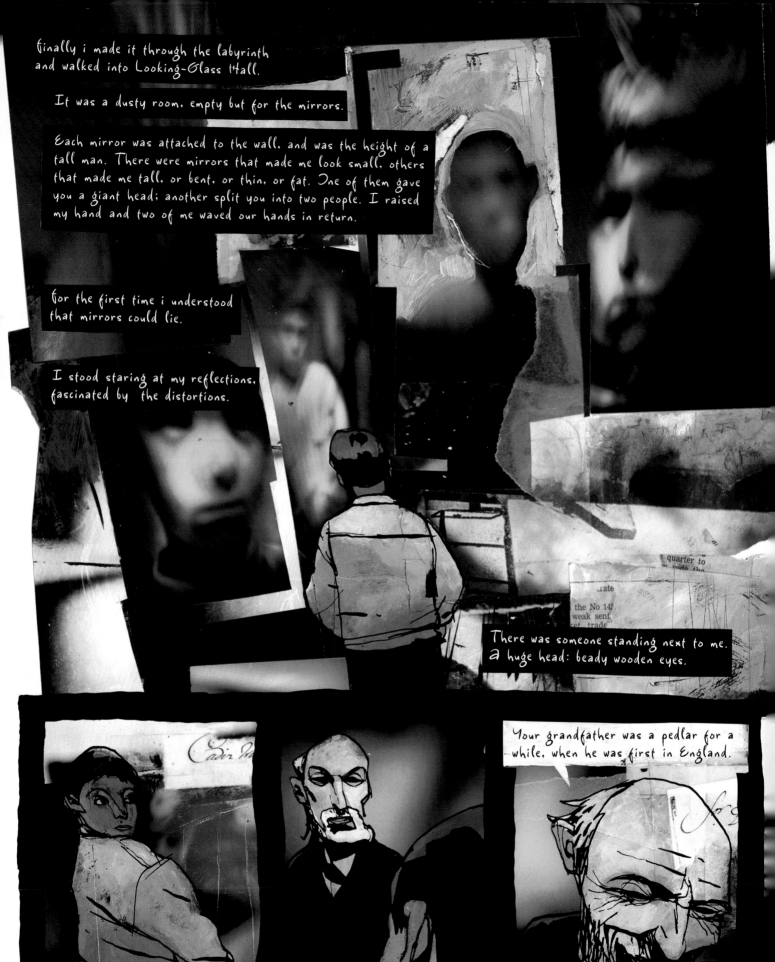

finally i made it through the labyrinth
and walked into Looking-Glass Hall.

It was a dusty room, empty but for the mirrors.

Each mirror was attached to the wall, and was the height of a
tall man. There were mirrors that made me look small, others
that made me tall, or bent, or thin, or fat. One of them gave
you a giant head; another split you into two people. I raised
my hand and two of me waved our hands in return.

for the first time i understood
that mirrors could lie.

I stood staring at my reflections,
fascinated by the distortions.

There was someone standing next to me.
a huge head: beady wooden eyes.

Your grandfather was a pedlar for a
while, when he was first in England.

1816.

"He was selling Sunlight Soap. Only it wasn't _real_ Sunlight Soap. It was a fake - a cheap carbolic soap. Rip the skin right off your face, it would.

"He walked from village to village. Or maybe he had a horse and cart. It'd gone by the time i met him, a-course.

"He was in Wales when it all went wrong. It was March, or early April. This was between the wars. He was having a great time, selling soap to the miners' wives. They all wanted it you see, for their husbands; they came back from the pit pretty black.

"Everything was just marvellous till he got a turned around on the mountain roads. He doesn't speak Welsh, not your grandfather. And those towns have long Welsh names - one looked pretty much like another.

"So one day he found himself back to a village he'd been to a week before. That was what made him give it all up."

Why?

"Because they near beat his breath from his body. That was where i found him.

"With a bar of soap in his mouth and bloody bubbles running down his face. You had to laugh.

"I was travelling back towards London. I always like to do a show in May in Covent Garden. Old times. Memories. So he came with me.

"He was my bottler."

My grandfather?

Best one i ever had.

I had hopes for your grandfather. He was a smart lad. Maybe he could have carved his own puppets. Made something of himself.

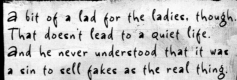

a bit of a lad for the ladies, though. That doesn't lead to a quiet life. and he never understood that it was a sin to sell fakes as the real thing.

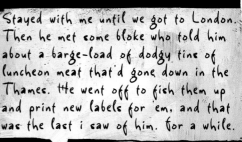

Stayed with me until we got to London. Then he met some bloke who told him about a barge-load of dodgy tins of luncheon meat that'd gone down in the Thames. He went off to fish them up and print new labels for 'em, and that was the last i saw of him. for a while.

I saw your grandfather again when i came through Portsmouth before the war. Owned four grocery shops he did. He'd done very well for himself.

That was a bad time for Punch and Judy professors, the last war.

Did they make you go in the army? Did you have to shoot people?

It wasn't that. They closed all the beaches. Put up barbed wire, and landmines and such. If you went on the beach you'd be killed.

We stepped over the last mirror, and walked out into the arcade once more.

Hey, boy. What do you want to be when you grow up?

I don't know. Shouldn't you be doing a show?

No. I'm finished here. There's only one more show to do in this place. And it won't be this afternoon, neither. Your grandfather's going to have to close the place down. Fire everyone. Won't be nobody at all here, tomorrow

The rain had stopped. I sat and read my comic for the second time. in the doorway. by the Punch and Judy theatre.

My Uncle Morton came out of the Arcade.

Do you want a ride back?

He owned a small bookmakers. which must. i suppose. have done fairly well. I remember the pattern in the bookmaker's window. abstract coloured shapes that hid the interior. It is still there. although his name has not been above the door for twenty years.

It was closed. He unlocked the front door and ushered me inside.

I walked around, staring at the blank television screens and the sporting prints on the walls. Morton walked behind the counter and opened a wall-safe, with a key.

He took a thick sheaf of notes from the safe, and closed the door behind him. He bound the money with a rubber band, and placed it in an envelope.

We drove down to a part of town i had never been before, filled with long rows of thin red-brick houses. Rusting cars on bricks sat in small, weed-filled front gardens, and people stared at us from behind dusty brown lace curtains, as we drove slowly down the road, looking for the house number.

I was disappointed; i had hoped to see him twirl a wheel, listening for the click of falling tumblers, like people did on television, or in books.

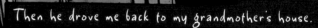

Then he drove me back to my grandmother's house.

He made me wait in the car, while he went up to a house and rang the doorbell. A woman opened the door: I couldn't see her face. He gave her the envelope full of money.

My grandmother was pleased to see me, and waved me in, urgently: my father had telephoned. I had a baby sister. What did i think of that, then? Was i excited?

I don't remember what i said. But, no, i wasn't excited.

I was never excited.

I slept soundly that night, and had no dreams that i have ever remembered.

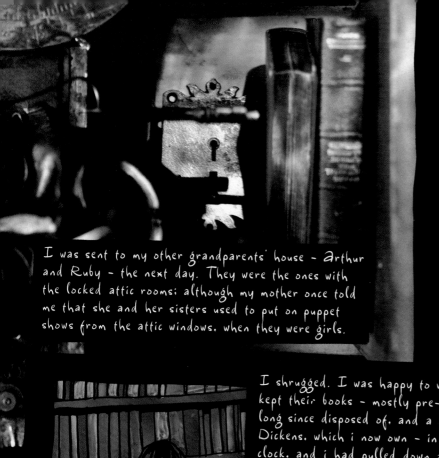

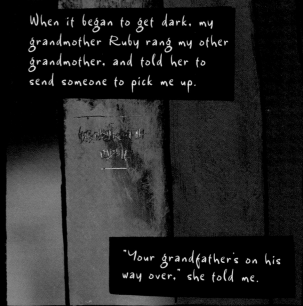

When it began to get dark, my grandmother Ruby rang my other grandmother, and told her to send someone to pick me up.

I was sent to my other grandparents' house – Arthur and Ruby – the next day. They were the ones with the locked attic rooms; although my mother once told me that she and her sisters used to put on puppet shows from the attic windows, when they were girls.

"Your grandfather's on his way over," she told me.

I shrugged. I was happy to wait. Arthur and Ruby kept their books – mostly pre-war *Reader's Digests*, long since disposed of, and a dusty bound set of Dickens, which i now own – in a shelved-in grandfather clock, and i had pulled down a copy of *The Old Curiosity Shop*, which was keeping me engrossed.

Eventually, my grandfather arrived. He didn't apologise for being late or anything. He just parked outside and hit the horn. I ran out, leaving, at my grandparents' insistence, the book behind me.

The seats of the Daimler were covered in old red leather. It smelled of leather and cigarette smoke.

My grandfather drove to the darkened arcade. "You wait here," he told me. He took a key-chain from his jacket pocket, and unlocked the door to the arcade. He went in.

In the darkness of the old car i sat and waited. I was bored.

I was cold.

My bladder began to feel uncomfortably full.

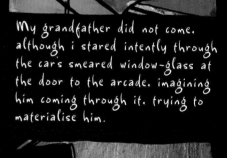

Rain began to fall, rattling on the roof. I wished i had been allowed to bring the book with me. If i had a book i would have had an escape hatch.

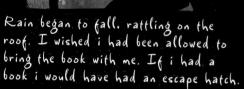

My grandfather did not come. although i stared intently through the car's smeared window-glass at the door to the arcade. imagining him coming through it. trying to materialise him.

No good. a driving rain was banging on the roof and windows of the car. and i could see almost nothing. I crossed my legs, hard, and then realised it was almost too late even for that.

I opened the door and ran for the light above the arcade door. as fast as i could. The rain soaked my hair and legs and face as i ran.

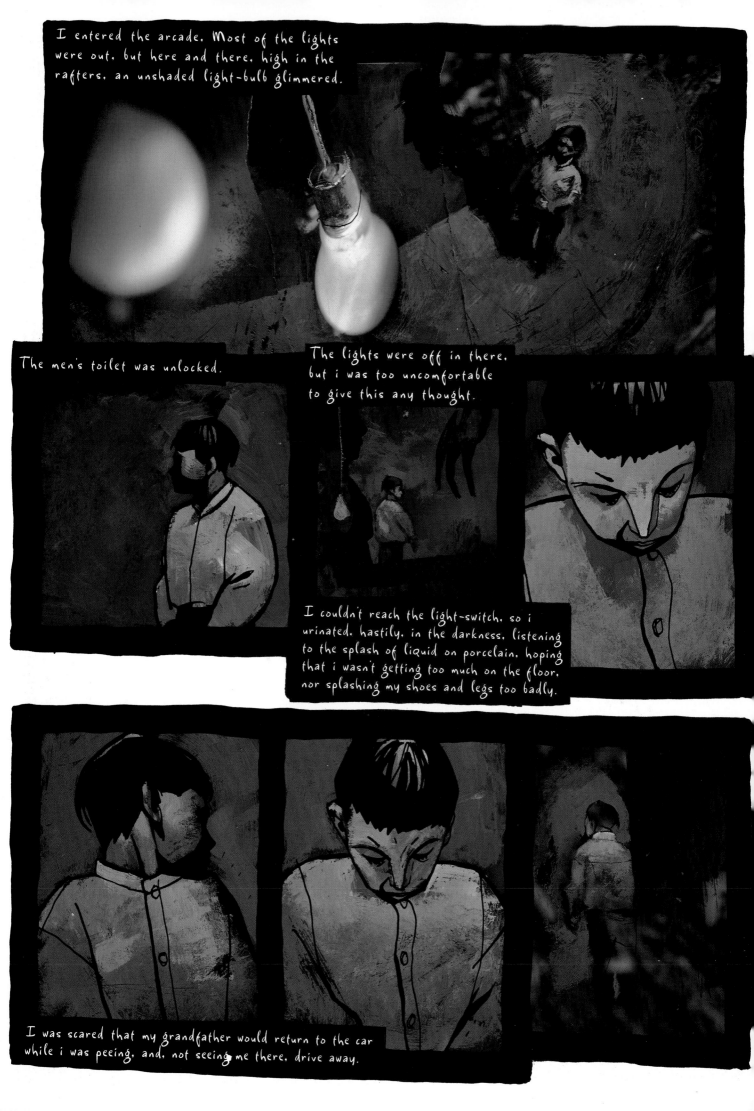

I entered the arcade. Most of the lights
were out. but here and there. high in the
rafters. an unshaded light-bulb glimmered.

The men's toilet was unlocked.

The lights were off in there.
but i was too uncomfortable
to give this any thought.

I couldn't reach the light-switch. so i
urinated. hastily. in the darkness. listening
to the splash of liquid on porcelain. hoping
that i wasn't getting too much on the floor.
nor splashing my shoes and legs too badly.

I was scared that my grandfather would return to the car
while i was peeing. and. not seeing me there. drive away.

Standing in the light were three men i recognised. and a woman that i didn't.

They were shouting, back and forth.

I was scared.

No, that's the wrong word. I wasn't scared, i was troubled. I wanted to run down and tell them to stop shouting, because it was upsetting me.

The woman pointed at one of the men, then, and began to laugh.

It was a nasty, contemptuous noise, in some ways more disturbing than the shouting had been.

The man picked up a slat of wood and began to hit the woman with it.

Once in the stomach.

Once across the face.

Another man pulled him off her.

She pulled herself to her feet. and let out one low scared whimper.

She ran, then, and none of the men tried to stop her.

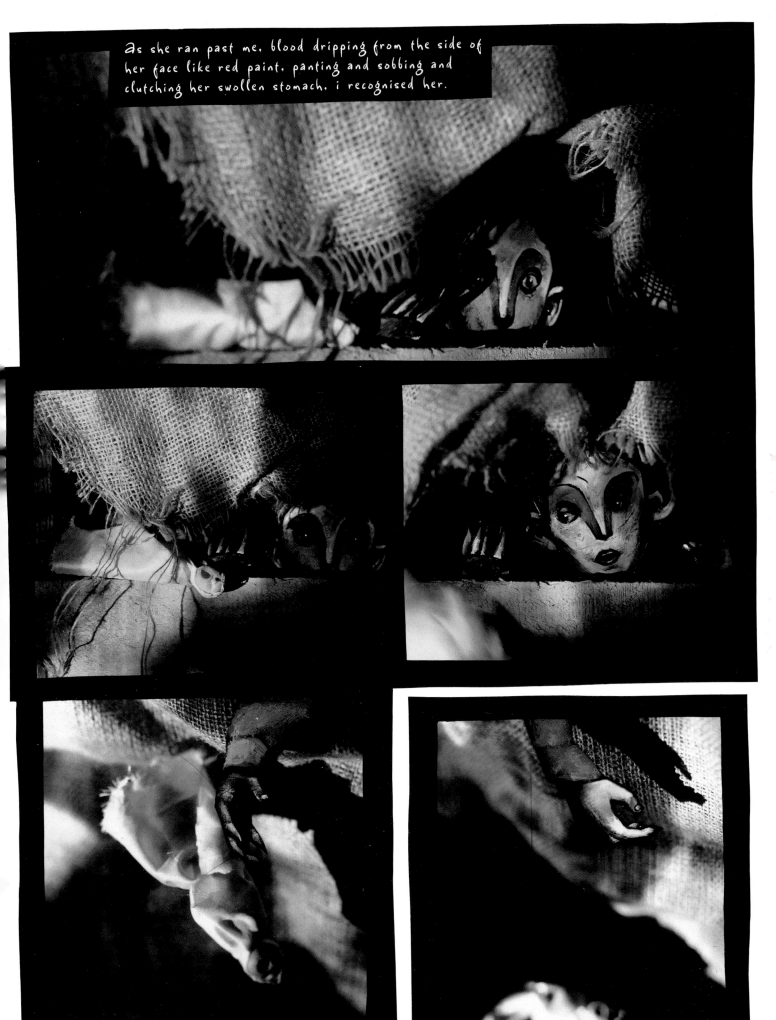

As she ran past me, blood dripping from the side of her face like red paint, panting and sobbing and clutching her swollen stomach, i recognised her.

I walked down the stairs to the place where the men had been.

If there <u>had</u> been three men, two of them were gone.

Only my grandfather was there, now. He was sitting on the floor, and he was crying, in deep, gasping sobs. His nose was running, and huge wet hot tears ran down his unshaven cheeks.

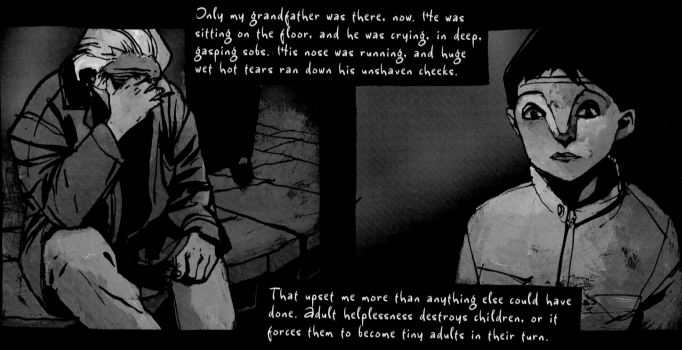

That upset me more than anything else could have done. Adult helplessness destroys children, or it forces them to become tiny adults in their turn.

He looked up, but I knew, somehow, that he was not seeing me properly.

He called me by my father's name, and reached out a hand to me. I helped him to his feet, and together we walked towards the car.

I was named after his father, who had died shortly before i was born. It was the custom.

At last he turned to me, and called me by my own name.

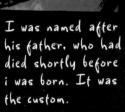

You didn't see anything.

he said.

He was telling me, not asking me.

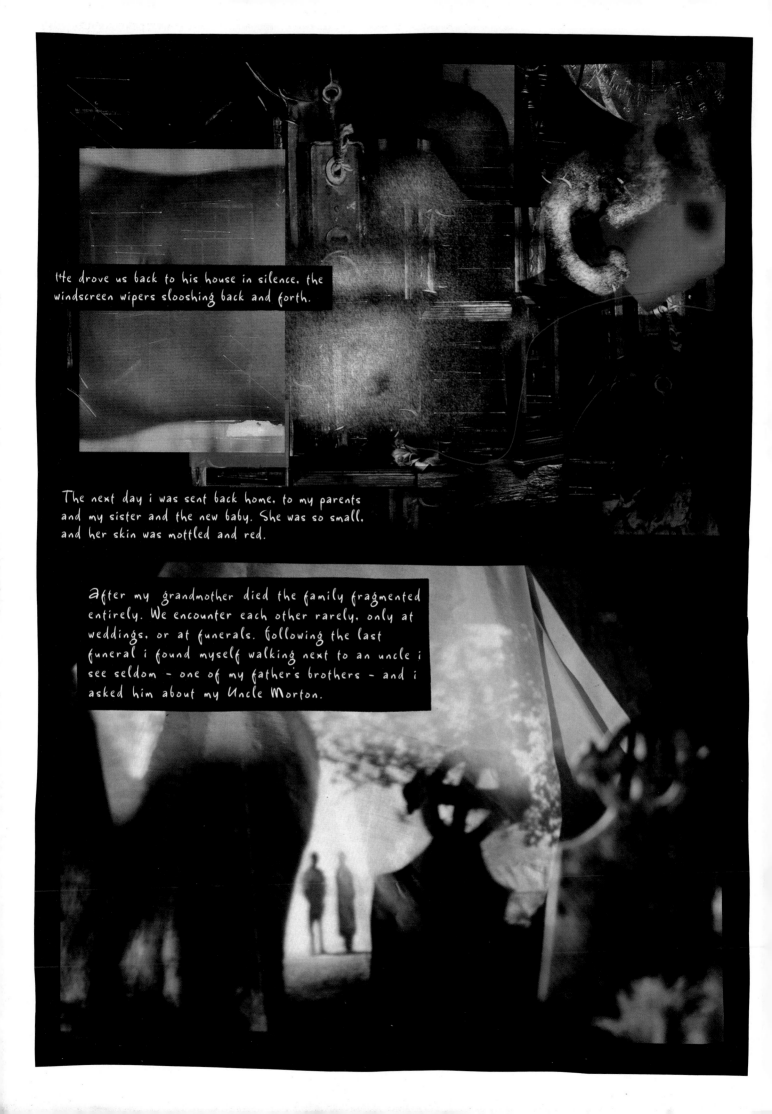

He drove us back to his house in silence, the windscreen wipers slooshing back and forth.

The next day i was sent back home, to my parents and my sister and the new baby. She was so small, and her skin was mottled and red.

After my grandmother died the family fragmented entirely. We encounter each other rarely, only at weddings, or at funerals. Following the last funeral i found myself walking next to an uncle i see seldom — one of my father's brothers — and i asked him about my Uncle Morton.

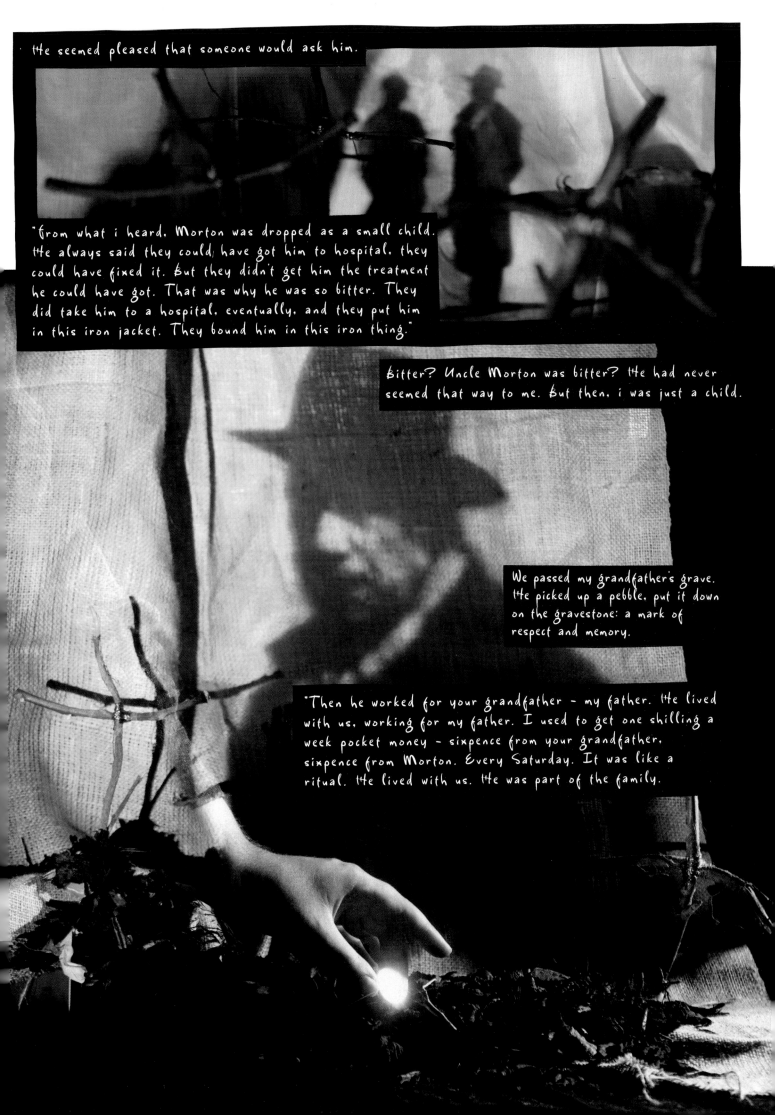

He seemed pleased that someone would ask him.

"From what i heard, Morton was dropped as a small child. He always said they could have got him to hospital, they could have fixed it. But they didn't get him the treatment he could have got. That was why he was so bitter. They did take him to a hospital, eventually, and they put him in this iron jacket. They bound him in this iron thing."

Bitter? Uncle Morton was bitter? He had never seemed that way to me. But then, i was just a child.

We passed my grandfather's grave. He picked up a pebble, put it down on the gravestone: a mark of respect and memory.

"Then he worked for your grandfather - my father. He lived with us, working for my father. I used to get one shilling a week pocket money - sixpence from your grandfather, sixpence from Morton. Every Saturday. It was like a ritual. He lived with us. He was part of the family.

"My father used to say... but he was a romancer. He used to romance. You'd have to take everything he said with a pinch of salt. Or more than a pinch. He used to say he was a twin. That he'd had a twin brother. Maybe he had, and maybe he hadn't.

"But there were no records, when they were little. You didn't want to keep records, they'd put you into the Russian army."

That was what he told me. That my grandfather was a romancer.

I don't know what the truth was. I am not even sure that i care. They're all dead, save possibly the Punch and Judy man, and i should let them rest.

My Uncle Morton died shortly after my grandfather. I was too young to go to his funeral, and if i was ever told how he died, i have long since forgotten.

Of course, he was old.

My grandfather, as i have said, went mad, although i did not realise that until much later. At the time, all i knew was that he was in hospital. It seemed like he was there for many years, but it could not have been that long. There was a wicker basket that he gave to my sister, which he had woven himself in some handicrafts class: it seemed a pitiful thing for my grandfather to have to do.

My father took us to see him. He was waiting for us, fully dressed, in the hospital waiting room, and we took him out for a drive down the sea-front. It was the middle of winter, and everything was closed, and the sea and the sky were grey as death.

Eventually we found a small tobacconist's where they also sold ice-creams and sweets.

My father bought us all ice-creams and we stood in the chilly wind on the sea-front and ate them, and shivered, and listened to the distant crash of the sea and the noise my grandfather made as he coughed and hawked up phlegm into a wad of discoloured tissues.

That was the last time i saw him.

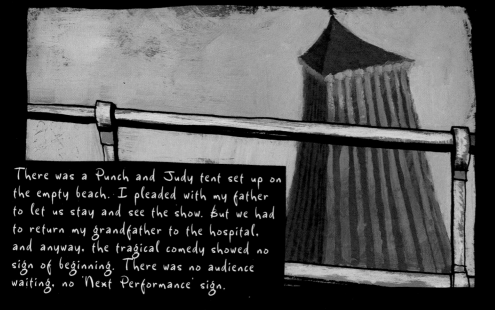

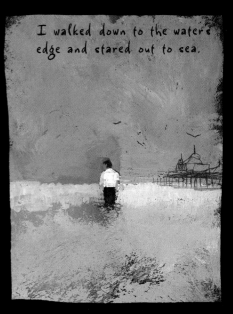

I walked down to the water's edge and stared out to sea.

There was a Punch and Judy tent set up on the empty beach. I pleaded with my father to let us stay and see the show. But we had to return my grandfather to the hospital. and anyway. the tragical comedy showed no sign of beginning. There was no audience waiting. no 'Next Performance' sign.

There was a woman, swimming, out in the Channel, despite the cold.

I thought perhaps she waved at me. but she was a long way off. and the cold wind made my eyes sting and go blurry;

When I'd blinked away the tears she was gone.

We finished the ice-creams and threw the sticks away, and took my grandfather back to the hospital.

They were hearts; you can't get them any more.

I thought i saw the Punch and Judy man a year ago last May, in a churchyard in Covent Garden. They celebrate Mister Punch's birthday there, and Punch and Judy professors come from all over the country to tell his story. The church even invites Mister Punch into the pulpit to read the lesson, in his squeaky, secret voice. I wonder what the Devil thinks of the arrangement - but i am sure he has spoken from the pulpit or the lectern in his time, also.

I had been watching a Victorian production of Punch and Judy in the churchyard. The puppets were old and elegant, and the puppet theatre, one of perhaps two dozen erected that day between the ancient gravestones, was elegantly carved out of wood, with hangings of blue velvet.

The beadle was attempting to hang Mister Punch.

Now, Mister Punch. You are going to suffer.

I don't want any supper!

You have to put your head into the loop.

I don't want any soup!

Just put your head in here.

Not that - that's yer arm. - Not that, that's yer other arm. Why, this is yer head.

Will you show me how to do it?

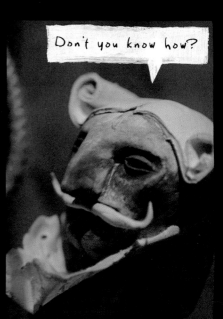

Don't you know how?

A hundred different performances of the comical tragedy were enacted that day.

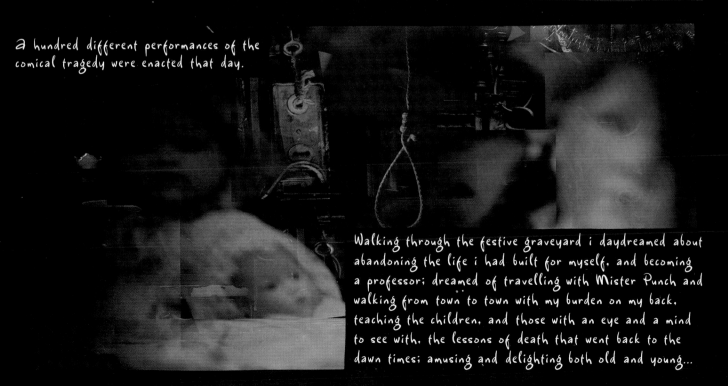

Walking through the festive graveyard i daydreamed about abandoning the life i had built for myself. and becoming a professor: dreamed of travelling with Mister Punch and walking from town to town with my burden on my back. teaching the children. and those with an eye and a mind to see with. the lessons of death that went back to the dawn times: amusing and delighting both old and young...

It was then that i saw him.

Later it occurred to me that the man i saw could not have been Swatchell. Nobody lives for ever, after all: not even the Devil. Everybody dies but Mister Punch, and he has only the life he steals from others.

I asked one man. who sold puppets and books from a table. whether he was familiar with a Professor Swatchell. He smiled. and showed me a small contraption. made of cotton and tin and tape: a swatchell.

When he placed it in his mouth he spoke with Punch's voice.

He placed the swatchell on the table in front of me.

You're not a professor then, sir?

I shook my head.

Would you like to try him on?

I almost put it on. It would have whispered its secrets to me. explained my childhood. explained my life...

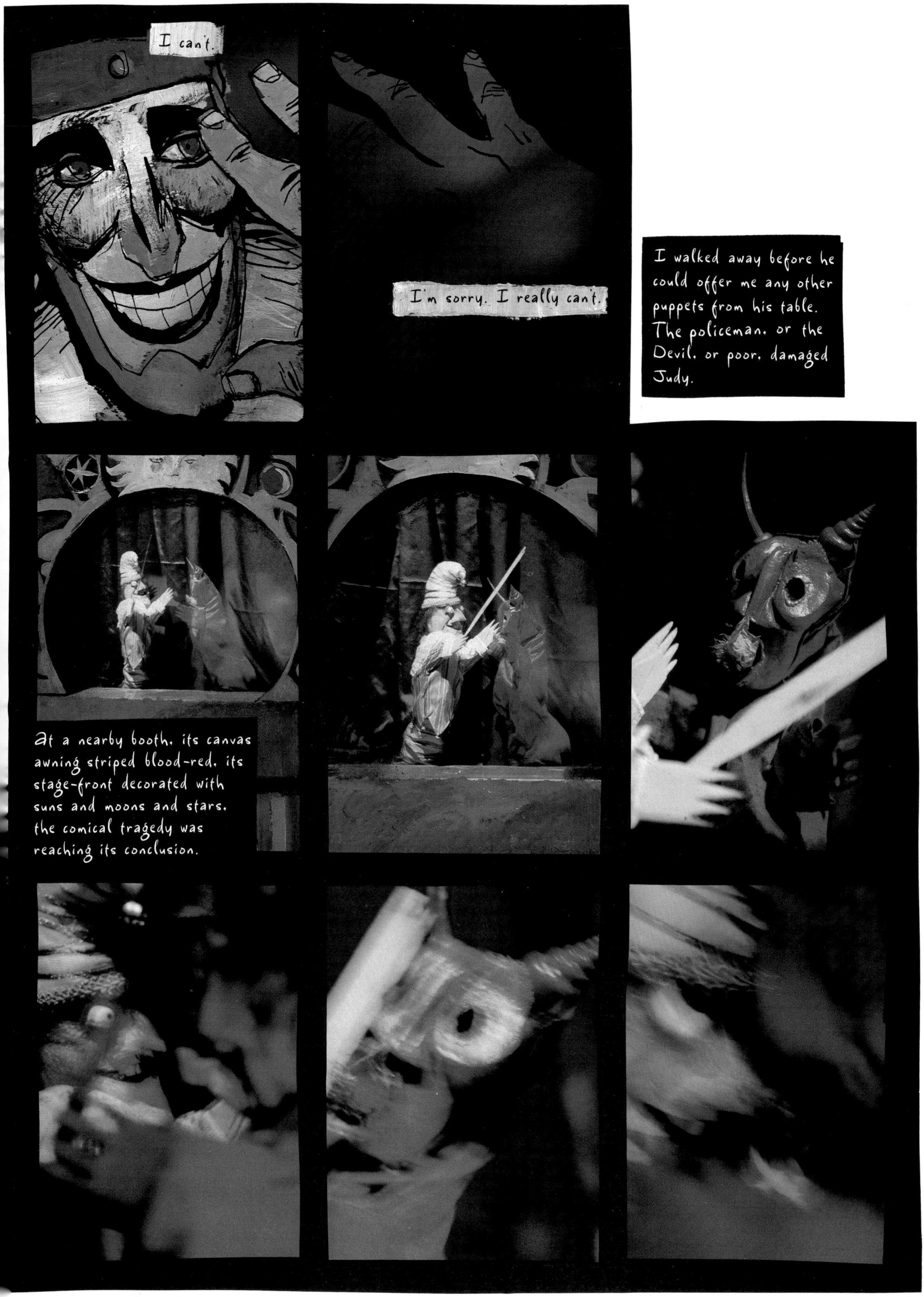

I can't.

I'm sorry. I really can't.

I walked away before he could offer me any other puppets from his table. The policeman, or the Devil, or poor, damaged Judy.

At a nearby booth, its canvas awning striped blood-red, its stage-front decorated with suns and moons and stars, the comical tragedy was reaching its conclusion.

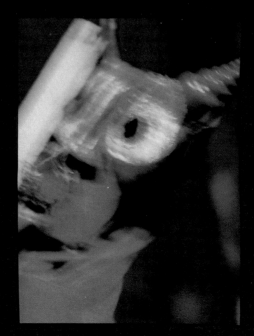

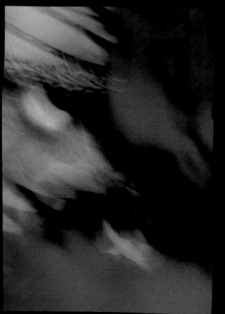

HOORAY!

HOORAY!

THE DEVIL IS DEAD

Now everybody is free

to do whatever they wish!

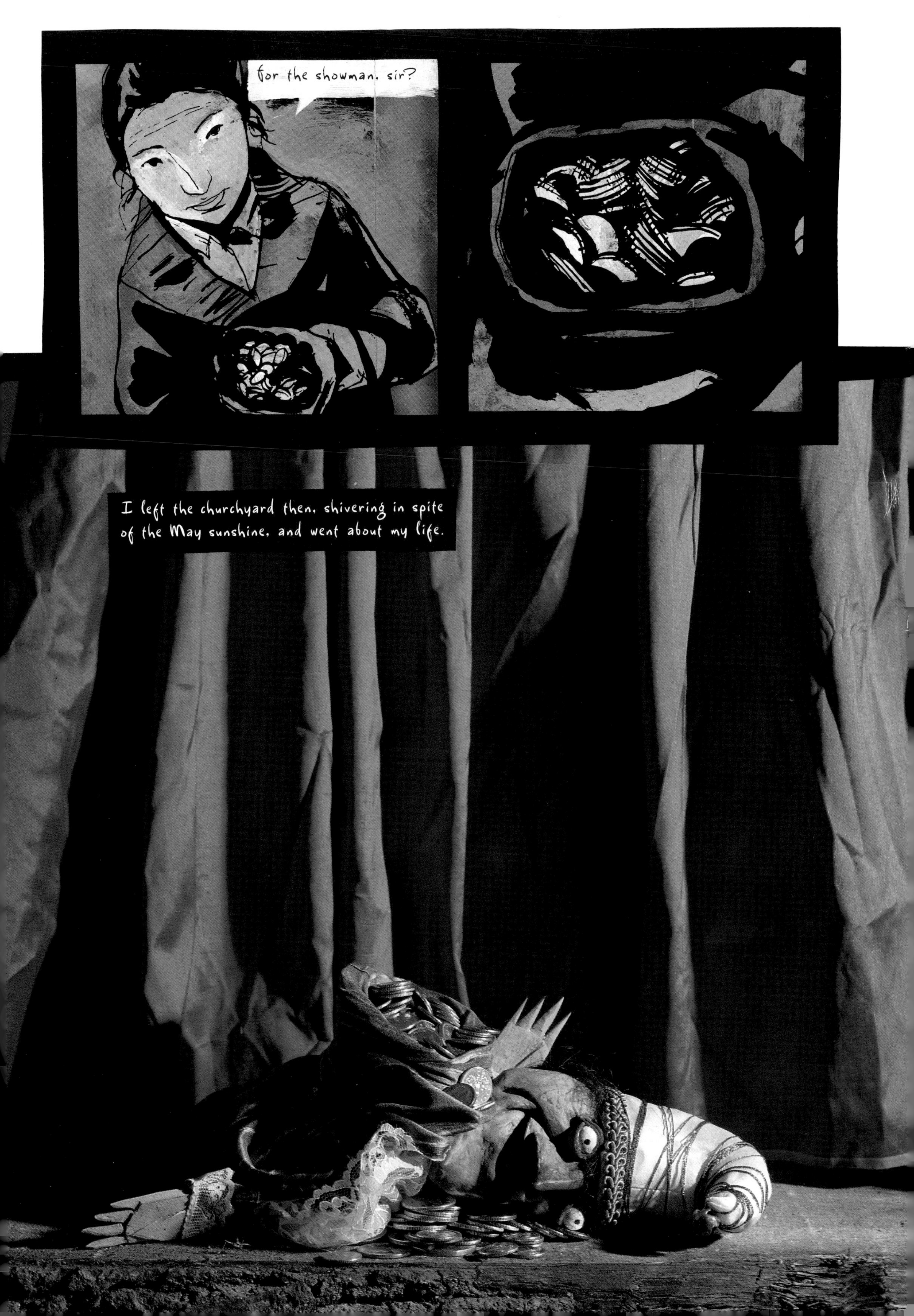
for the showman, sir?
I left the churchyard then, shivering in spite of the May sunshine, and went about my life.

Neil Gaiman

was born in November 1960. He lives in an odd, rambling house of uncertain location, where he writes in a basement room filled with books and old armchairs. He has two cats, who are both quite mad, and two children, who are, to his occasional surprise, fairly sane, and a very nice wife. He has received a number of awards, and, while he no longer believes that being a grown-up is all it's cracked up to be, still enjoys staying up after his bed-time.

Dave McKean

is a regular contributor to the New Yorker magazine, frequent designer/illustrator/ photographer for C.D. and book covers, and is currently writing as well as drawing the irregular, infrequent five-hundred page serialized comic novel 'Cages' (although it should be done by now). He has won many awards, exhibited in Europe and America, and now lives in the Kent countryside with partner Clare and new-born storm-in-a-teacup Yolanda, who has, together with Clare and Kent, inspired much of this book.